GLORY DAYS

London Trolleybuses

Glyn Kraemer-Johnson & John Bishop

Ian Allan
PUBLISHING

Front cover:
Could be titled 'April showers'! At the western extremity of route 657 at Hounslow, all-Leyland Class K1 No 1117 (EXV 117), dating from 1939, turns for the return trip to Shepherds Bush. BMC cars and the common Pearl Assurance advertisement complete this tranquil Sunday scene recorded in April 1962. *John Bishop*

Back cover:
Altogether 150 Class K1 all-Leyland trolleybuses were delivered, numbered from 1055 to 1154 and 1255 to 1304. No 1058 (EXV 58) was an early example, seen at Isleworth depot in April 1962. By this time there were only two depots; Isleworth was the Leyland domain whilst Fulwell housed the last AECs. Within four weeks this fine-looking vehicle would be withdrawn. *John Bishop*

Title page:
No 954, seen near the end of its life approaching Barnet on route 609, was the second chassisless (as opposed to unit-construction) vehicle to run for London Transport, using AEC/Metrovick running units on an Metro-Cammell body, and took the classification 'L2'. It was easily recognisable because the cream relief band continued below the windscreens. *N. Rayfield / Lawrie Bowles collection*

CONTENTS

Acknowledgements

The authors would like to acknowledge the following publications, which have been helpful in researching this book:

The London Trolleybus (Dryhurst Publications, 1961)
London's Trolleybuses — A Fleet History (PSV Circle/Omnibus Society, 1969)
Trolleybus by Ken Blacker (Capital Transport, 1975)
London Trolleybus Routes by Hugh Taylor (Capital Transport, 1994)
London Trolleybus Chronology by Mick Webber (Ian Allan Publishing, 1997)
The London Trolleybus 1931-1945 by Ken Blacker (Capital Transport, 2002)
London Transport Magazine (various issues)

The photographers whose work has been used have been acknowledged wherever known.

Narrative by Glyn Kraemer-Johnson
Photographs selected and captioned by John Bishop

"...And the constant click and kissing of the trolley buses hissing"

from 'Harrow-on-the-Hill' by Sir John Betjeman

First published 2003

ISBN 0 7110 2949 0

© Ian Allan Publishing Ltd 2003

Published by Ian Allan Publishing

an imprint of Ian Allan Publishing Ltd, Hersham, Surrey KT12 4RG.

Printed by Ian Allan Printing Ltd, Hersham, Surrey KT12 4RG.

Code: 0309/B1

INTRODUCTION

My life was saved by a courteous London trolleybus driver.

During World War 2 I lived at Horns Cross, near Dartford, and my maternal grandparents lived at Bexleyheath. The journey to visit them usually entailed an STL, often of the front-entrance variety, on route 480 to Dartford Market Place, followed by a 696 trolleybus to Bexleyheath Broadway. One such journey, taken when I was about four, is etched on my memory.

It was a dark winter's evening. My mother and I left my grandparents' house as usual and walked to the bus stop where we would catch our 696. As we turned the corner into the Broadway a trolleybus was just drawing away from the stop. My mother began to run, holding up her hand and the driver brought the bus to a halt, allowing us to board. I clearly remember sitting on the long seat inside the door. As we approached the Clock Tower, there was a vivid blue flash, which we took to come from the overhead. "Everybody down!" shouted the conductor. I remember crouching in the gangway and hearing a muffled crump in the distance.

Some time later we learned that the 'crump' had been the sound of a bomb falling on the very bus stop at which we would have been waiting had that courteous driver not stopped for us to board. I've often wondered whether this incident provided some Freudian reason for my subsequent interest in buses. It certainly gave me an affinity to the London trolleybus.

Another picture from around the same time was of a very early morning, around six o' clock I think, arriving at Market Street, Dartford, to catch a 696 trolleybus to Woolwich, where my Granddad worked as a marine engineer. He'd arranged for us to take a tour of the aircraft carrier *Campania*, although how he managed to arrange it in wartime I'll never know. I was very impressed by the ship, especially by the myriad of gauges and dials in the engine room. However, my most enduring memory of the day was not of the aircraft carrier but of standing in Dartford Market Place, shortly before it was light, watching those massive trolleybuses gliding into view with hooded interior lights and masked headlamps, their approach almost silent apart from the faint hum of the motor — an all-round eerie experience. And then on board, climbing to the top deck, full with dockers and workers from the Vickers factory at Crayford, all smoking and creating an atmosphere that could have cured kippers.

There are many other memories that come to mind. Those huge bench seats for five on the lower deck, the purring of the compressor, the strange smell that was unique to trolleybuses, not only those in London. I remember standing at a bus stop and watching the wires begin to twitch, heralding the approach of a trolleybus. I remember the chirping of the overhead and the clicking of the points — Sir John Betjeman's 'click and kissing'.

Whether it was because I was most familiar with the Bexleyheath routes where there were possibly fewer junctions I don't know, but I remember only rarely seeing a London trolleybus dewired. When later I moved to Brighton dewirements seemed a very common occurrence, but then, to my young eyes Brighton's weren't real trolleybuses; they only had four wheels.

In a sister volume on Southdown buses, John and I set the Glory Days period as being from 1929, with the introduction of the Leyland Titan, to 1969, when the National Bus Company was formed. With the exception of a few early experiments, that same period covers the entire life of the trolleybus in London, so this book will attempt to tell the story of the London trolley from beginning to end. It is not intended to be a precise history — that has already been done — nor does it purport to be a technical volume. Rather, it is an informal look at the largest trolleybus system in the world, the vehicles it operated and the places it served from its birth to its premature and untimely death. Like most operations, during their lifetimes vehicles and services were altered from time to time. Our descriptions of both routes and trolleybuses are as they were at their inception, and only major subsequent changes are recorded.

Unfortunately, unlike its predecessor the tram, the trolleybus has enjoyed no reincarnation. When the last trolleybus ran through Croydon no one imagined that, some 40 years later, its place would be taken by trams, so perhaps it is not too fantastic to envisage that in years to come those silent servants might once again be seen on the streets of London.

Glyn Kraemer-Johnson
Hailsham, East Sussex
April 2003

1. ENTER THE 'DIDDLER'

▶ It is hardly surprising that the trolleybus was so readily accepted as a replacement for the tram; at the time, the differences between the two modes of transport must have seemed vast.

For those too young to remember, the trams of the 1930s and '40s were a far cry from the sleek articulated monsters that glide through the streets of our cities today. They were, with a few exceptions, ponderous, swaying, noisy giants which hogged the centre of the road, even at stops, delaying other traffic and causing boarding and alighting passengers to risk accident and injury from other road users. Further delays were caused at certain points where 'change pits' were located and where conductors would disembark to change the tram from overhead to conduit operation or vice-versa. They were frequently draughty, often with open balconies exposing the driver to the elements, and, in many cases, open-top, so that passengers too were unprotected from wind, rain and snow.

The trolleybuses, when they arrived, were smooth, virtually silent in operation, and could manœuvre their way around other traffic and pull into the kerb at bus stops while still attached to the overhead. And, of course, there was no track to maintain (or to trap the wheels of unwary cyclists!). Hardly surprising, then, that, once adopted, the trolleybus spread quite rapidly.

There had been several experiments in the London area, but it was London United Tramways that introduced the first trolleybus into revenue-earning service. Ironically, the area chosen for the initial tram replacement was that around Wimbledon, the suburb which would see the rebirth of the London tram some 70 years later.

The first public service was operated on 16 May 1931 between Teddington and Twickenham, using the first of 60 trolleybuses that were to become known affectionately as the 'Diddlers'. The reason for this nickname is not clear. One explanation is that it is a corruption of the word 'tiddler', whilst an item in the London Transport house magazine suggested that their appearance 'diddled' the public into believing they were motor buses. Whatever the true reason, the name seems a very apt one and

conjures up pictures of these busy little vehicles 'diddling' around the Kingston and Twickenham areas.

A month later, with the arrival of more trolleybuses, the route was extended to Kingston-on-Thames and, in July, a new service (2) was introduced between Tolworth and the Dittons, running around the Tolworth loop in an anti-clockwise direction. Journeys operating in the clockwise direction were numbered 3. This was the first of a number of trolleybus routes to be given different numbers according to their direction of travel.

The final stage of the first tram-to-trolleybus conversion scheme came about in September, when route 4 was introduced between Wimbledon and Hampton Court, although trams continued to operate for a few weeks longer until sufficient trolleybuses had been delivered to work the full service.

The vehicles purchased by LUT for this initial conversion were built on the AEC 663T six-wheel chassis, which was basically similar to the Renown motor-bus chassis then being purchased in quite large numbers by the London General Omnibus Co as its LT class. As on the Renown, the motor (obviously electric in this case) was housed beneath a bonnet at the front of the vehicle, which resulted in the trolleybus's being built to the half-cab design.

The 'Diddlers' were delivered in two batches over a period of 12 months, being numbered 1-60 and given non-matching two-letter registration numbers in the HX, MG and MV series, the numbers being in no particular sequence. They were split into two classes — A1 (Nos 1-35) and A2 (36-60). The main difference between the two classes was that the 'A1s' had electrical equipment manufactured by the English Electric Co, whilst that on the 'A2s' was from British Thomson Houston (BTH). The equipment fitted to the 'A1s' included English Electric six-notch controllers, which made their acceleration lively, to say the least. The 'A2s' had nine-notch controllers, making their 'take-off' a little more sedate.

The contract for building the bodies was given to the Union Construction Co, a company which had been formed specifically to build a fleet of Underground cars and was currently engaged in building the famous 'Feltham' tramcars. The parentage of the 'Diddlers' was immediately apparent, especially in the domed roof over the driver's cab, which was pure 'Feltham'.

In fact the bodies were a strange mixture of ancient and modern. Their half-cab design, retrospectively at least, made them look almost prehistoric when compared to the smooth lines of the full-fronted trolleys that followed. The bonnet design underwent several changes, and there were several variants amongst the first few buses delivered. It originally carried a grille, almost like an elongated Routemaster grille, but this was eventually replaced by two rows of horizontal slats between which was fitted a single headlight. Had they earned the nickname 'Cyclops' it would have been quite logical!

The driver was provided with a very narrow windscreen, an angled window being fitted between it and the cab door, the latter being something not normally found on London buses of the time.

Another of the eccentricities found on the original 'Diddler' was the front destination display. This consisted of four boards, triangular in elevation, which have been likened to today's Toblerone chocolate packets. A destination was painted on each of the three faces of each board, and they were swivelled into place to show the desired display. The route number was simply a metal stencil fitted to the front of the roof, which must have

caused some inconvenience (if not actual back injury) to the conductor, who had to change it by leaning backwards out of the front upper-deck window.

Before the buses entered service they were fitted with conventional roller blinds at front and side, although these were still unusual in showing the route number in black on a white rectangle. The rear display, however, consisted simply of a board showing the ultimate destination, which was carried in the rear platform window. This window too was something of an oddity; on No 1 it was unglazed and on the next few examples was glazed but with a 4in gap at the top. Full glazing was fitted later.

The idea of using a six-wheel chassis arose from a desire to maximise seating capacity, bringing it as close as possible to that of a tram — something the 'Diddler' failed to achieve. This was partly due to the fact that it was fitted with a large platform and a straight staircase (a layout then popular with London General on its LT- and ST-class motor buses); this inevitably

reduced the length of the offside longitudinal seat on the lower deck and the number of seats that could be accommodated on the offside of the upper deck. Seating capacity was thus reduced to 56, with 24 seats on the lower deck and 32 upstairs. The last of the batch, No 60, was given a curved staircase, which reduced the platform area but could have allowed for an increased seating capacity. This opportunity was not taken, however, and the capacity remained at 56, although with a different arrangement of 29 upstairs and 27 down.

The interior was quite luxurious and owed much to the 'Felthams'. Window surrounds were of an unusual silver-grey wood. The lower-deck side panels were covered in blue rexine with the plush seats being upholstered in grey moquette. On the upper deck both seats and side panels were in red.

When new the 'Diddlers' were painted in the standard LUT livery of red below the lower-deck windows and 'broken white' above, with black lining-out. Following the formation of the London Passenger Transport Board they were repainted red with cream upper-deck window surrounds and two cream bands, one above and one below the lower-deck windows.

Aside from the occasional loan to another depot for driver-training purposes or to cover vehicle shortages, Nos 1-60 spent their entire working lives operating from Fulwell depot. A start would be made on their withdrawal in 1948, by which time they had provided excellent service 'diddling' around the Tolworth, Kingston and Hampton Court areas.

By 1933 trolleybus design was proceeding apace. AEC had produced an entirely new trolleybus chassis in which the motor was placed below the floor, thus allowing a smoother, more modern, full-fronted body to be fitted. The chassis was still designated 663T, but the wheelbase was extended from 16ft 6in to 18ft 7⅜in. This allowed for a body to the then maximum length (for six-wheelers) of 30ft to be fitted, which in turn would permit a seating capacity of 70, a figure much nearer to that of the tram.

In March 1933 LUT took delivery of a similar chassis, but designated 691T, on which was mounted an LGOC body — the only trolleybus body to be wholly built at Chiswick. In fact the entire vehicle was to remain unique, as no other 691T chassis were ever built. The new trolleybus was a far cry from the 'Diddlers' and bore more than a passing resemblance to the double-deck AEC Q types that were to follow it out of Chiswick a few months later. It had a gently curving frontal profile with full-width cab and featured a centre entrance with power-operated doors; an emergency door was fitted at the rear of the lower deck. The seating capacity was raised from the conservative 56 of the 'Diddlers' to a much more acceptable 74. Although the bus had a full-width cab, only half of this was occupied by the driver, there being to his left a longitudinal seat for five that extended back to the doorway. Internally its Chiswick parentage was more apparent, in the extensive use of rexine in place of varnished

wood. The lower-deck ceiling and light fittings were also of the standard Chiswick pattern.

Numbered 61 (AHX 801) and classified 'X1', the new trolleybus entered service on the Wimbledon–Hampton Court route at the end of March 1933. It was the last trolleybus supplied to the LUT which, three months later, became part of the newly formed London Passenger Transport Board; in fact, it was never actually owned by LUT, being on loan from AEC until it was purchased by the LPTB in March 1934.

Few of London's trolleybuses travelled far from the capital, but No 61 made two trips to the South Coast. In 1933 it was taken to Bournemouth, where it was inspected by delegates at the Electrical Convention. Three years later it travelled to Brighton, where it was demonstrated to members of the Transport Committee who were considering the replacement of the town's trams with trolleybuses. Like the 'Diddlers', however, it spent most of its life working from Fulwell depot. Towards the end of World War 2 it was used in London Transport's 'Pay As You Board' experiments, which are described in a later chapter.

Delivered only 15 months after the last 'Diddler', No 61 (AHX 801) represented a massive leap forward in design, incorporating features which would endure until the UK's last trolleybuses were withdrawn in 1972. With chassis by AEC and bodywork by the London General Omnibus Co (LGOC), it bore an unmistakable resemblance to the AEC Q-type motor bus. Classified 'X1' (and thus always considered experimental), No 61 would survive until September 1951.
Glyn Kraemer-Johnson collection

2. THE BOARD TAKES OVER

London also experimented with a two-axle AEC chassis, bodied by English Electric, but No 63 (AXU 189), classified 'X3', would always be the odd man out. In this undated photograph, taken during its time allocated to Isleworth depot, it heads for Brentford on a short working of route 657. By this time it had undergone various changes to its destination screens, the original standard design having given way to a four-screen layout and finally that depicted. *C. Carter*

Upon its formation in July 1933 the LPTB had inherited a massive, ailing tram system, a mixed fleet of buses and a small trolleybus system in the Kingston area of South West London. The Board eventually decided on a policy of replacing the trams with trolleybuses and thus had to settle on a standard design. In 1934 it took delivery of two vehicles, of which No 62 (AXU 188) set the seal on London trolleybus design for the next 18 years. With chassis by AEC and bodywork by Metro-Cammell, it was classified 'X2' in the experimental series. Seen in postwar days at Holloway on route 653, it would survive until June 1952. *C. Carter*

▶▶ Even before the London Passenger Transport Board came into being on 1 July 1933 there were rumours that one of its first tasks would be to replace the tramway system, probably with motor buses. It soon looked as if this assumption had been correct when buses began to replace trams on some of the more unremunerative services, such as Dartford–Horns Cross, Dartford–Wilmington and Oak Grove–Penge. However, LUT's trolleybuses were proving a success — a fact not overlooked by the LPTB, which, in November 1933, announced that a Bill was to be placed before Parliament seeking to replace the older and less economic tramways with trolleybuses, the services in question being mainly in South East and South West London. Powers were also sought to build a new trolleybus depot at Bexleyheath to serve the Woolwich–Abbey Wood–Bexleyheath and Woolwich–Bexleyheath–Dartford services.

The Bill was passed by Parliament on 31 July 1934, and London Transport was empowered to begin its tramway

replacement programme, which in the event (due to one or two hiccups such as World War 2), would take almost 20 years to complete.

In anticipation of the Bill being passed, London Transport had already ordered two trolleybuses for evaluation purposes. The first of these, No 62 (AXU 188) was classified 'X2' and used the updated AEC 663T chassis, which, despite retaining its original designation, was now more akin to the 'one-off' 691T, with the motor mounted beneath the floor.

The body was built by Metro-Cammell, this time to a conventional rear-entrance layout. Again, although full-fronted, the bus had a half-width bulkhead behind the driver and to his left a longitudinal seat for three. Overall seating capacity was 73. The seats themselves had a curved top to each seating space, with a dip in between; what in my mind I call 'bra-shaped'! They had Metro-Cammell lightweight metal frames and were covered in green moquette with rexine-covered backs. Green rexine was also

used to cover the side panels and window surrounds. The use of rexine in place of varnished wood seems to have been one of the few areas where London Transport's preferences extended to the trolleybus fleet.

In researching this book we have constantly been struck by the fact that the Tram & Trolleybus Department operated virtually as an autonomous unit, and few of the standard motor-bus features were adopted as might have been expected. Livery, destination displays, lettering on destination blinds, seat and moquette design — all were different from those adopted as standard for the motor-bus fleet. Windows were square-cornered with spring-loaded half-drops, long after the 9T9s and RTs had standardised on the winding window with radiused corners. As for the overall design of the trolleybus, this never bore any relationship to contemporary motor-bus bodywork.

No 62, licensed on 6 July 1934, was clearly the prototype for the design that was to become London's standard and the basis, with only minor differences, for the 1,800-odd trolleybuses that were to follow. The design was modern and attractive, simple and unlikely to date, but it bore no resemblance to the contemporary motor bus, the STL. Studying the standard London trolleybus today, the only body it resembles is Leyland's own double-deck bus body, standard on the Titan chassis throughout the late 1930s, 1940s and 1950s. The resemblance is not accidental, for, in 1936, Leyland bodied its first batch of trolleybuses for London to the standard LT design. Leyland's engineers obviously approved of the design, for it was adapted to form the basis of their all-metal body introduced later that year and which, with some fairly minor modifications, would remain in production until Leyland ceased its bodybuilding activities.

Another view of No 63, showing the lines of the English Electric body to full advantage and emphasising how trolleybus design had developed in just three years. The original beading below the upper-deck windows, which carried cream livery when delivered, was never removed. Seen *en route* to Hampton Court on route 604, No 63 would be withdrawn in October 1952.
Glyn Kraemer-Johnson collection

Back to No 62. The body was of six-bay construction with an upward-sloping upper edge to the cab side windows, which was to become a characteristic of the subsequent trolleys. The front was virtually the same as the standard design, even down to the destination display. By this time the LGOC and subsequently the LPTB had standardised on the destination displays fitted to double-deck buses. These consisted of a three-aperture display at front and rear with separate route number and 'via-points' blinds above a single-line ultimate destination. It might quite logically have been expected that this layout would be used on the trolleybuses, but it was again indicative of the independence of the Tram & Trolleybus Department that a layout loosely akin to that carried by the trams was adopted. This consisted of a rectangular screen in which the ultimate destination and (usually) two lines of intermediate points were shown; above this was another rectangular box, slightly narrower, in which the route number was displayed.

Differences from the standard vehicles included a rear offside staircase window and smaller-than-usual rear upper-deck side windows. Sidelights were mounted on the waistband. The livery was red with three cream bands and a silver roof.

A month later, in August 1934, the second evaluation vehicle arrived in the shape of No 63 (AXU 189), which, not surprisingly, was classified 'X3'. Again, AEC provided the chassis, but this time it was of type 661T — the shorter, four-wheel version. The body was built by English Electric and, due to the shorter length, seated only 60. This bus also had a longitudinal seat beside the driver but for only two passengers. Seats were of the standard LPTB wooden-framed type.

Of all the experimental trolleybuses to operate in the capital, No 63 probably looked the least at home. Obviously its single rear axle immediately set it apart, but in addition the frontal profile was more curved and, in plan, more bowed. It lacked the metal louvres over the windows, which were a feature of all

A front offside view of Class C1 Metro-Cammell-bodied AEC No 142 (CGF 142) in original condition, showing (when compared with later photographs) how much the 'C1s' were modified over the years; as built they embodied a small window at the rear to lighten the stairs and a route-number stencil-holder at the rear, both of which were later removed. Note the sidelights in the cream area above the driver's cab and the space to the left of the cab where the passenger was able to sit by the driver — a schoolboy's dream! *Glyn Kraemer-Johnson collection*

subsequent trolleys and the rear profile was unusually upright. No 62 had a single-piece emergency exit that tapered inwards towards the top, and this was adopted as standard; on No 63 the emergency exit was divided. The latter also had sidelights positioned more conventionally, on the lower-deck waistband. It was also subsequently fitted with a rather flamboyant style of 'spats' on the rear wheels.

No 63's destination display was originally the same as that on No 62, but it was later given new destination boxes front and rear, consisting of a three-aperture display similar to (but shallower than) that on the STL motor bus, with the route number and 'via point' screens above a single-line ultimate destination. Above these three screens was a further single-line display in which appeared

◀ Stonebridge-allocated 'C1' No 180 (CGF 180) in postwar guise looks bare without front advertisements as it leaves North Finchley for Hammersmith on route 660 in the early 1950s. The famous Gaumont cinema in the background is now history, having been demolished in the late 1980s. *F. G. Reynolds*

the word 'TROLLEYBUS'. This was one of the few instances where the men at 55 Broadway endeavoured to bring trolleybuses into line with the motor-bus fleet, but the idea was opposed by the Trolleybus Department and eventually abandoned; the single-line apertures were panelled over, but the non-standard number and destination screens were retained, requiring special blinds to be made for the bus throughout the rest of its life.

Nos 62 and 63 both entered service on route 4 (Wimbledon–Hampton Court) in the autumn of 1934 for evaluation purposes. It was eventually decided that the six-wheel version was better suited to London's requirements, largely because its seating capacity was closer to that of the trams it was replacing, and four-wheeler No 63 thus remained unique.

As a result of the trials an order for 120 new trolleybuses was placed for the first stages of the tramway-replacement scheme. Although the experimental trolleybuses had all been of AEC manufacture, the initial order for production vehicles was shared

between AEC and Leyland, the former supplying 52 chassis and the latter 68.

Although not numerically the first, the AECs were in fact the first to enter service. Classified 'C1' and numbered 132-83 (CGF 132-83), they had the 664T chassis of 18ft 7⁵⁄₁₆in wheelbase and 70-seat bodies by Weymann (132-41) or Metro-Cammell (142-83) — a rare instance of buses from two different bodybuilders being included in the same class. These buses were the first to have matching fleet and registration numbers — something that would be perpetuated by all subsequent trolleybuses, with two exceptions,

In overall appearance the 'C1' was a 'cleaned up' version of No 62. There were only six windows on the offside of the lower deck, light to the staircase being provided by a small window at the rear, rather like the conductor's signalling window on the STL. The seating capacity was lower than that of No 62 due to the omission of the rearmost offside upper-deck seat and the reduction of the longitudinal bench beside the driver to take only two; the half-width front bulkhead was retained. Seats themselves were metal-framed with separate grab-rails, and these would remain standard for all subsequent trolleybuses, despite the development of a new standard seat for motor buses.

There were other, minor differences between the production vehicles and the prototype, such as the positioning of the rear number plate and the fitting of stylish rear mudguards, which were painted red. The 'C1s' were the first trolleybuses to be fitted with the familiar bell cord — something that would later be adopted as standard on the motor-bus fleet. The livery was also modified, being red with a cream waistband and a broader cream band below the lower-deck windows; the roof (rear dome aside) was silver. On front and rear lower panels and beside the platform they carried a stylised London Transport bullseye, in blue and gold, which incorporated a 'T' and the word 'TROLLEYBUS'.

The first routes to be converted by the LPTB were the 657 (formerly tram route 57), which ran from Shepherd's Bush to Hounslow Heath, and the 667 (tram route 67) from Hammersmith to Hampton Court. In the London Transport route-numbering scheme it had been decided that trolleybus routes would be allocated numbers in the 5xx and 6xx series and wherever possible would use the tram route number preceded by 5 or 6. The 657 was operated from Hounslow depot and the 667 from Fulwell, both depots saying goodbye to their trams and Hounslow being substantially rebuilt for its new role.

Meanwhile, the first Leylands were being delivered, and a dozen or so were sent to Fulwell to help with the conversion of route 667 pending delivery of sufficient AECs. The remainder went to a new purpose-built depot at Bexleyheath, where they were stored prior to the next stage of the conversion. Classified 'B1' and 'B2', they were numbered 64-93 ('B1') and 94-131 ('B2'), all with matching CGF registrations.

The cast was set in respect of design with the delivery of Class B1 with BRCW bodywork mounted on Leyland chassis, albeit short versions, compared with future deliveries. No 64 (CGF 64), numerically the first of the batch, is seen negotiating the roundabout under construction at Crystal Palace to assist trolleybuses turning there. Just visible behind No 64 is a tram, dating this view to 1935.
A. D. Packer /
The Omnibus Society

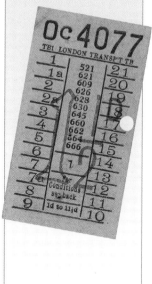

A fine prewar photograph taken at West Croydon, showing Sutton-bound 'B1' No 65 (CGF 65) in full LPTB livery, complete with short-lived silver roof. The trolleybus depot for route 654 was Sutton, subsequently renamed Carshalton. Behind is ST 1031, which came from Pembroke and carried a Birch Bros body. *The Omnibus Society*

Given the decision to standardise upon the six-wheel chassis in order to maximise seating capacity, it was perhaps ironic that the first (numerically, at least) materialised on a short-wheelbase (16ft 6in) version of the Leyland TTB2 chassis, seating only 60, albeit still with twin rear axles. The reason for this was that they were intended for use on routes with tight corners or awkward bridges, which might be difficult to negotiate with a longer vehicle. However, the Bexleyheath routes to which the 'B2s' were allocated encountered few (if any) such obstacles, and this, together with increased passenger loadings, later resulted in their being transferred to other parts.

The 'B1s' were bodied by the Birmingham Railway Carriage & Wagon Co (BRCW) and the 'B2s' by Brush of Loughborough. Externally, apart from the shorter length and the five-bay construction, there was little difference between these and the 'C1s', although the rear mudguards, still of the streamlined type, were shallower than those on the AECs.

By 10 November 1935 sufficient 'B2s' had been delivered to allow conversion of the route between Bexleyheath, Erith, Abbey Wood and Woolwich Free Ferry, as trolleybus route 698. This

was followed a fortnight later by the 696 from Dartford to Woolwich via Crayford, Bexleyheath and Welling, many parts of the route being quite rural. This put an end to the truly antiquated tramways being operated by Bexley, Dartford and Erith councils.

The 'B1s' were earmarked to replace the open-top tramcars which had originated with the South Met, the first conversion involving the introduction of the 654 between Sutton, West Croydon, Selhurst, Anerley and Crystal Palace. In the event, conversion took place in two stages, that between Sutton and West Croydon commencing on 9 December 1935. It was not until the following February that the section to Crystal Palace could be opened, when wiring had been completed and sufficient 'B2s' delivered; even then, a small number of 'Diddlers' were drafted in from Fulwell to help out, as, indeed, they had been at Bexley. The Crystal Palace terminus was approached via Anerley Hill, with gradients as steep as 1 in 9, and it was felt that additional safety measures were called for. The 'B1s' were thus fitted with coasting and run-back brakes, to prevent them from running away either forwards or backwards.

A photograph which speaks volumes, when one invested in Britain or you could buy 'Chef Sauce' for a shilling (5p)! The CN (Carshalton) depot code is plainly seen on the nearside of Class B1 No 70 (CGF 70). Note the radio suppressors clearly seen against the skyline on the roof and 'National Benzole Mixture' long gone from our petrol forecourts. *Alan B. Cross*

From this rear offside view of Class B1 No 81 (CGF 81) one can see the 'TROLLEYBUS' transfer on the rear window which proudly stated the type of vehicle. A BRCW-bodied Leyland, it stands at the set-down stop at the top of Anerley Hill, having arrived from Sutton. The conductor has already changed the blinds for the return journey. For the area the 'B1' class were fitted with coasting and run-back brakes as added safety measures. The shortness of the body can be seen by the five-bay window layout rather than the standard six-bay layout which would become standard for further 'normal' deliveries.
F. G. Reynolds

Even before the Bexleyheath and Crystal Palace routes had commenced operation, powers had been sought for a further 16 routes to be converted, this time in North and East London, and orders placed for another 570 trolleybus chassis, with bodywork by a variety of manufacturers. Once again the chassis order was to be divided between AEC and Leyland, whilst amongst the bodybuilders were BRCW, Brush, Leyland, MCW and Park Royal. It seemed that the advance of the trolleybus was unstoppable.

Following the conversions in South West and South East London, the LPTB turned its attention to the North West for the next stage of the tram-replacement programme. In April 1936 new trolleybus route 660 was introduced, running between Hammersmith and Acton and operated by Acton depot. The route was very short-lived, being replaced in July by new service 666, running between Hammersmith and Edgware via Acton, Willesden and Cricklewood and worked by Acton, Hendon and Stonebridge depots. The following month route 660 was reintroduced, this time running between Hammersmith and North Finchley, and, at the same time, new route 645 was introduced between North Finchley and Edgware. Hard on the heels of these routes came the 662 and 664 between Paddington Green and Sudbury (662) or Edgware (664), operated from Acton, Hendon, Finchley and Stonebridge, tram routes 62, 64 and 66 being withdrawn as a result.

All the new routes were worked by newly delivered AEC trolleybuses of Classes C2 and C3. Two hundred of these had been ordered in July 1935, delivery commencing in March 1936. All were based on the AEC 664T chassis with English Electric equipment, the 70-seat bodies being supplied by either Metro-Cammell (Class C2) or BRCW (C3); they were numbered 184-283 and 284-383 respectively and had corresponding CUL registrations. Although they were basically similar to the 'C1s', there were several differences, the most noticeable being the fitting of red-painted streamlined rear mudguards, which covered the top third of the wheels. Many have said that these 'spats', as they became known, added the final touch to an already handsome body; in this writer's opinion they detracted from the vehicles' attractive lines, but then beauty is a very personal thing. In any case, London Transport had second thoughts on the matter,

and only the first 99 (49 'C2s' and 50 'C3s') were so equipped, after which more conventional black rubber mudguards were fitted, these being less susceptible to damage. However, those first 99 retained their spats throughout their lives, and I remember being quite flabbergasted the first time I saw one in the mid-1950s.

Northeast London had not yet featured in the tramway-replacement programme, but this was corrected on 18 October 1936, when trolleybus route 623 replaced tram route 23 (Woodford–Ferry Lane). However, the trolleybus route was extended beyond the tram terminus to Tottenham Hale and on to the Piccadilly Line Underground station at Manor House. 'C3s' were used for the conversion.

From North East London the hungry trolleybus returned to the West in search of its next prey. This turned out to be close to its roots in former LUT territory. On 15 November 1936 tram route 7

▲ Allocated to Stonebridge, Class C2 AEC/Metro-Cammell No 185 (CUL 185) shows the spats covering the top of the rear wheels, giving a stylish finish to the design. Note also that the sidelights on this vehicle are in the standard position on the lower panels. The spats would be retained until withdrawal in 1955, No 185 finally ending up at Bird (dealer), Stratford-upon-Avon, in May 1956. *F. G. Reynolds*

from Shepherd's Bush to Uxbridge became trolleybus route 607, operated by Hanwell depot, although trolleybuses were housed initially at Acton, pending the completion of building works. In a way this stage of the programme was a sad one, for the 7 was one of the most heavily trafficked LUT routes, and the trams being replaced were the modern 'Felthams', although these were, of course, transferred to other areas.

A new class of trolleybus was introduced to work the 607. Back in April 1936 another of London's 'one-off' trolleybuses had been delivered. Numbered 384 (CUL 384), it was to be the sole member of Class D1 and was in actual fact the prototype for Leyland's own version of the London trolleybus body. It was also the first 30ft Leyland to be built for London. Again, it was very similar to the AECs, but there were minor differences; No 384 featured the streamlined spats over the rear wheels and would be the only Leyland so fitted. The body itself differed in some of its dimensions, the most noticeable being the depth of the panels between the waistband and the upper-deck windows, this being deeper than on its predecessors, the upper-deck windows being shallower as a result.

No 384 was allocated originally to Bexleyheath, but after 12 months or so it was returned to Leyland for modifications and never returned to Bexley. Presumably there were a few aspects of

the Leyland body which did not meet the Board's standards, for a further 99 Leylands ordered with Leyland bodywork had this changed to Metro-Cammell. These 'D2s' were numbered 385-483 (DGY 385-483). Although initial deliveries were to Hanwell and Acton, 'D2s' were also allocated to Bexleyheath, where they replaced 60-seaters; they were, indeed, the buses I remember as mostly operating on the 696. The bodies on these vehicles were obviously very similar to those of the 'C3s', although there were again minor differences, such as deeper rainshields over the windows.

At about this time there arrived a further 10 short-wheelbase 60-seaters. When ordered, these were intended to augment the allocation of 60-seaters at Bexley, but, before they had been built, permission had been granted for 70-seaters to operate from Bexley, and these 10 vehicles were therefore virtually redundant even before they were delivered. Like the 'B1s', they were Leylands with BRCW bodies, but the first five,

This photograph possibly explains why London Transport discontinued the silver roofs, judging by the staining. Seen in the Docks on route 685 to Crooked Billet, Class D2 Leyland/Metro-Cammell No 398 (DGY 398) is very much in original condition, with full chrome around the cab glass. *The Omnibus Society*

As 1936 drew to a close London turned to Leyland for chassis construction with the Class D2. Ninety-nine were built, of which a number were based at Bexleyheath in Kent. Although very much a satellite system, not being connected to the rest of London's trolleybus network, this did not prevent flying bombs from striking the depot. One such casualty of hostilities was No 390 (DGY 390), seen postwar as 390B after rebodying by East Lancs. *D. A. Jones*

An immaculate Class D2 Metro-Cammell-bodied Leyland trolleybus, No 417 (DGY 417), at journey's end in Dartford, Kent. The 696 was very much out on a limb from the rest of the system, and from Dartford one would have to continue one's journey east by Country Area bus. Trolleybus poles would remain in this locality for over a decade after closure of the system. *London Trolleybus Preservation Society*

A sight more familiar to Dartford enthusiasts in the late 1950s, when there were always at least three vehicles in view. Leyland/Metro-Cammell Class D2 No 471 (DGY 471) prepares to depart on the 696 to Woolwich, after which the next vehicle will move forward. The Fremlins advertisement adds a local touch, this being a Kent brew now long gone.
A. B. Cross

The interior of London's trolleybuses was always very functional but comfortable nevertheless. Even as a child one could see out of the front window! Looking forward in Class D2 No 470B (DGY 470), rebuilt by East Lancs after war damage, we see the driver, in full London Transport uniform with white-topped cap, eyeing the photographer in his mirror! The advertisement above the bulkhead, promoting an Erith company, gives that local feel.
A. B. Cross

Another view of the interior of No 470B, looking towards the rear and the long bench seat over the rear twin axles and showing the upholstery pattern. The transfer on the rear window leaves no doubt that this vehicle is a trolleybus! On the rear lower panel London Transport went so far as to describe it as a Class D2, repainted in May 1956. *A. B. Cross*

Nos 484-8 (DGY 484-8), lacked coasting and run-back brakes and were therefore classified 'B3'. For the final five, 489-93 (DGY 489-93), the specification was changed to include coasting and run-back brakes, and these were thus classified 'B1'.

Nos 484-93 were also noteworthy as being the last complete batches of trolleybuses delivered with a half-width cab. Experience had shown (although it seems to have taken a long time to do so) that passengers using the longitudinal seat beside the driver not only restricted his vision but were also a distraction. It must certainly have been off-putting for the driver to have passengers staring at him throughout their journey, especially as this seat would likely have been the one for which children made a bee-line. Most trolleybuses subsequently had this seat removed and the bulkhead extended across the full width of the bus, the space to the left of the driver being used to house the traction batteries as well as becoming the usual storage space for the driver's flask and sandwiches.

Towards the end of 1936 tram route 55 was replaced by trolleybus route 655 from Hammersmith to Hanwell Broadway via Ealing and Acton, worked by 'D2s' from Hanwell. On the other side of London, tram route 85 became trolleybus route 685 on 17 January 1937, running between Crooked Billet and Markhouse Road, later being extended to Canning Town; for this service surplus 'C3s' were allocated to Walthamstow.

The trolleybus really made inroads into the East End six months later with four new services. The routes concerned were the 669 from Stratford Broadway to Canning Town and the 687, 697 and 699, all of which operated from Chingford Mount to the Victoria and Albert Docks but by different routes: the 687 via Wanstead Flats, the 697 via Abbey Arms and the 699 by way of Greengate Street. Apart from the 669, worked by West Ham alone, these services were operated jointly by West Ham and Walthamstow depots.

For these conversions the remaining 'D2s' were dispatched to West Ham, along with the five 'B3' 60-seaters. Three new classes of trolleybus were also involved, these being the 'E1s', numbered 554-603, 'E2s', numbered 604-28, and 'E3s', numbered 629-53, all with matching DLY registrations. The 'E2s' and 'E3s' were all sent to West Ham together with some 'E1s', the remainder of which were allocated to Walthamstow.

All three 'E' classes were mounted on the now-familiar AEC 664T chassis, the 'E1s' having the last Brush bodies to be supplied to London Transport, the 'E2s' being bodied by Weymann and the 'E3s' having the first London trolleybus bodies to be built by Park Royal. Again, there were slight differences in the Brush bodies when compared to earlier examples, notably the squared-off top to the driver's cab door. Externally the Weymann bodies of the 'E2s' were virtually indistinguishable from previous

ones built by Metro-Cammell, but internally, along with the 'E1s' and 'E3s', they introduced a new colour scheme of mustard and brown, with seat moquette to match. The Park Royal-bodied 'E3s' were easily identifiable by their thick front upper-deck corner panels and flatter front rainshields. The Weymann and Brush bodies were well built but those built by Park Royal, somewhat surprisingly for a manufacturer that was to become one of the major suppliers of London buses, deteriorated badly, mainly from corrosion and body distortion, and all would be withdrawn and scrapped by 1956.

By far the largest conversion to date, and one that affected both East and West London, took place on 12 September 1937. New trolleybus routes included the 626 (Acton–Harlesden–Hammersmith–Clapham Junction), 628 (Craven Park–Harlesden–Hammersmith–Clapham Junction) and 630 (Scrubs Lane–West Croydon), which saw the end of tramway operation in West London. All were operated by Hammersmith depot, using 14 brand-new trolleybuses of Class D3, delivered from May 1937;

At the beginning of 1938 London Transport commenced withdrawal of the Barking and Ilford trams. Class E1 AEC No 587 (DLY 587), with Brush bodywork, stands on redundant tram track covered with a token quantity of tarmac. The 692 route operated between Ilford and Chadwell Heath on a Saturday-only basis but was very short-lived, lasting only until December 1938. Close scrutiny of the shops behind reveals advertisements for Lyons' Ice Cream 2d (1p) and Cherry Blossom shoe polish!
C. F. Klapper / The Omnibus Society

these were Leylands with BRCW bodywork and were the last trolleybuses delivered with polished windscreen surrounds. They were numbered 494-553 and were the lowest-numbered of a new registration series of matching DLY marks, although this had actually been introduced with the first 'E3s' in March. In South London, route 612 was introduced between Battersea and Mitcham over former tram route 12. This was the first time that a tram route using the conduit system of current collection had been involved, the conversion being more costly and complicated and necessitating the erection of completely new overhead for trolleybus operation. The 612 was worked by Wandsworth depot, using 'D2s'. In East London the 689 commenced, using 'E'-class vehicles from West Ham depot and operating a circular route linking Stratford Broadway and East Ham; however, buses showing the same destinations but running in opposite directions caused some confusion, and in December the anti-clockwise journeys were renumbered 690.

Delivered concurrently with the 'D3s' and the 'E' classes was the 100-strong 'F1' class, numbered 654-753 (DLY 654-753). These were again Leylands but with Leyland's own bodywork — that originally ordered for the 'D' class. The bodies were generally similar to those which had gone before, but, like

Two Class E1 Brush-bodied AECs, the first being No 601 (DLY 601) and that behind No 597, stand at Barking terminus in 1938, by which time the polished surrounds to the cab windows had disappeared from new deliveries. The driver of No 601, in smart white uniform, appears still to be feeling his way around this new mode of transport! When this photograph was taken the Ilford/Barking routes were still isolated from the rest of the system. *C. F. Klapper / The Omnibus Society* ▲

An official photograph of Class E3 No 641 (DLY 641) in absolutely pristine condition prior to delivery in 1937. Featuring Park Royal bodywork on AEC chassis, the 'E3' class was relatively small, numbering just 25 vehicles. Five would be rebuilt after enemy bombing, including No 641, rebodied by Northern Coachbuilders and gaining a 'C' suffix. *Glyn Kraemer-Johnson collection* ▶

Class D3 Leyland No 504 (DLY 504), with BRCW bodywork, seen prewar against a backdrop of terraced houses and roads deserted save for an American car parked on the corner at route 612's 'Prince's Head' terminus at Battersea — an act calculated to provoke any traffic warden if repeated today! *C. F. Klapper / The Omnibus Society*

Under the right circumstances all three types of road-based public transport could be encountered in this area of Battersea, where trolleybuses met up with trams and buses. Here we see Class D3 Leyland No 518 (DLY 518), in prewar guise complete with silver roof, when almost new on route 612; about to overtake is an STL-class AEC Regent, while in the foreground are conduit tram tracks for routes to Wandsworth. *The Omnibus Society*

Leyland provided both chassis and bodywork for Class F1, introduced in 1937 and comprising 100 vehicles. Upon delivery the whole class was allocated to Hanwell depot for the 607 and 655 routes, No 676 (DLY 676) being depicted at Acton Vale *en route* to Shepherds Bush c1959. *R. H. G. Simpson*

Seemingly oblivious to the march of time symbolised by construction of the flyover above, Class F1 No 680 (DLY 680) passes Chiswick *en route* for Hanwell Broadway on route 655 in 1960. The 655 had the distinction of extensions at either end — to Clapham Junction in the south and Acton in the west — for special journeys. *R. H. G. Simpson*

No 384, the solitary 'D1', they were deeper between decks and had a narrower cream waistband. They stood up well to London service, and the Leyland body gained a good reputation. They also had more powerful Metrovick motors, of 95hp instead of the 80hp specified hitherto. The 'F1s' were allocated to Hanwell depot, which had been completely rebuilt for its new role and had replaced the now-closed Acton. To complete the conversion, 61 'D2s' were transferred from Acton to Hammersmith, where they joined the 'D3s'.

Following on numerically from the 'F1s' was No 754 (DLY 754), the first of a number of 'chassisless' trolleybuses to enter the London fleet. Built by London Transport at Charlton Works, it incorporated AEC running units and was classified 'X4'. The integral has definite advantages, its construction resulting in a more rigid vehicle less likely to suffer from distortion and warping, and a lower height can be achieved without sacrificing headroom in either saloon. It also makes for some weight saving (about 6cwt in the case of No 754). However, No 754's construction was not its only remarkable feature. In addition to

the normal open rear platform, it had a front exit fitted with jack-knife doors. This resulted in the loss of four seats, but two were reclaimed by reintroducing the half-width bulkhead and fitting a bench seat for two facing the driver. No 754 could be easily identified, not only from the nearside, where the front exit was a give-away, but from the offside as well, the reason being that the cream waistband was in fact a metal strip which was fixed to the body and which carried no black lining. The bus spent its entire working life at Finchley depot. The front exit was not a success and fell into disuse in later years.

During 1937 another large order was placed, favouring both AEC and Leyland, the new vehicles starting to arrive in February 1938 and introducing yet more new classes to the fleet.

These consisted of the first of 150 Leylands with Metro-Cammell bodies, classified 'H1', the complete class being numbered 755-904, with matching ELB registrations. On these buses the power cables were fed through the first upper-deck window pillar, resulting in this pillar being wider than the rest — a feature that became standard on subsequent London trolleybuses

Class H1 No 810 (ELB 810) stops in Plumstead High Street on the main-road run to Bexleyheath and Dartford. The first 'H1s' were originally allocated to Highgate, but war munitions work in the Woolwich area saw the transfer of a number, including No 810 as here, to Bexleyheath. No 810 would be one of the early withdrawals of this class, in December 1955. *A. B. Cross*

Class H1 Metro-Cammell-bodied Leyland No 815 (ELB 815) nears journey's end at Moorgate in the late 1950s. This scene presages times to come, with cars scattered around, but Congestion Charging was still more than 40 years away, and at this time trolleybuses were blamed for the congestion. The Austin Cambridge and Morris Minor have a nostalgic appeal today but cannot outclass the 'H1'. *R. H. G. Simpson*

The 1936-9 period can be regarded as the glory days, when the trolleybus in London seemed unstoppable. Parliament Hill Fields, South End Green, was the terminus of the 513/613 route. In this prewar scene almost-new Class J2 BRCW-bodied AEC No 1026, with red roof, lays over as 'H1' Leyland No 792, with silver roof, inches up behind. The tram track is by now redundant, while the STL has taken its rightful place behind the bushes!
C. F. Klapper / The Omnibus Society

Heading north towards Enfield, Class J2 No 981 (ELB 981), a BRCW-bodied AEC of 1938, forms part of a typical London scene featuring a 'Steptoe & Son' horse-and-cart and a rather forbidding-looking public house. This was a time when everything was functional and replaced only when worn rather than for fashion's sake.
C. F. Klapper / The Omnibus Society

and was also to be seen on most provincial trolleys; when Doncaster transferred some Roe bodies from withdrawn trolleybuses to new motor-bus chassis, this thick pillar was the most obvious sign of their origin. The 'H1s' also introduced 'louvred' grilles (or, as Del Boy might have said, 'lowvried grilles') in place of the wire grilles used previously.

Next came 48 AEC 664Ts, of which 47 (Nos 905-51) were bodied by Weymann, the final one (952) receiving a body by Metro-Cammell identical to that carried by the 'H1s'. All were classified 'J1' and had ELB registrations. Delivered concurrently was the 'J2' class, again on AEC 664T chassis but with bodywork by BRCW. They were numbered 955-1029 and registered ELB 955-99, EXX 10 and EXV 1-29; like that of RM1000 which was to follow, the registration of trolleybus 1000 was a 'one-off'.

'What', I hear the more observant ask, 'happened to 953 and 954?' The answer is that these numbers were taken by two experimental vehicles.

No 953, delivered in 1938, was the first of the 'M1' class and was the first trolleybus built by a method known as 'unit construction'. Put very simply, this meant that the bus had a conventional chassis but with out-riggers that coincided with the body pillars, thus giving a rigid construction without the need for the usual floor cross-members. It also showed a saving in weight. No 953 had a Weymann body and was the first London trolley to have radiused top corners to the front upper-deck windows. It also incorporated a single-piece front destination screen without the usual division between route number and destination. Unfortunately this handsome vehicle was destroyed by fire in 1943. Although LT would not persevere with unit construction beyond the production batch (1530-54), this would later be used successfully on many provincial buses, including the Bristol Lodekka.

The second experimental vehicle was a development of 'X4' No 754 and was, coincidentally, numbered two hundred higher as 954 (ELB 954). This again was of chassisless construction, but this time built by Metro-Cammell incorporating AEC running units and using methods resulting in a more rigid construction. Outwardly it was little different from the 'H1s' but could always be readily identified by the cream band below the lower-deck windows, which continued around the front of the vehicle below the windscreen. It was classified 'L2'. Experience gained with 754 and 954 resulted in orders being placed for a further 175 of the type.

Back to the conversion programme, and the next stage took place on 6 February 1938, when Ilford depot lost its trams in favour of 'E1' trolleys. The routes concerned were:

691 (ex-tram 91)	Barkingside–Barking
692 (new route)	The Horns–Chadwell Heath (Saturdays only)
693 (ex-tram 93)	Chadwell Heath–Barking

March 1938 witnessed the removal of the remaining trams from Finchley, one consequence of which was the allocation of trolleybuses to Holloway, eventually to become London's largest trolleybus depot. The same month also saw trolleybuses running into the heart of London as far as Holborn. The routes in question were:

609	Barnet–Moorgate
517/617	North Finchley–Highgate–Holborn
521/621	North Finchley–Finsbury Park–Holborn
651	Barnet–Cricklewood

This was the first use of the 5xx series and denoted the direction of travel around the Holborn loop, the 6xx series running in a clockwise direction and the 5xx series anticlockwise. The vehicles used were 'J1s' and 'J2s' allocated to Finchley and 'H1s' to Holloway. This stage of the conversion programme was particularly sad for the tramway enthusiast, as it witnessed the removal of the ultra-modern 'Felthams' to the South, where they operated until their untimely departure to Leeds.

'J1s', 'J2s' and 'H1s' were again used for the next conversion, in May 1938, which brought trolleybuses as near to the West End as Tottenham Court Road and saw the end of tramway operation from Wood Green. The replacement trolleybus services were:

625	Woodford–Wood Green
629	Tottenham Court Road–Enfield
641	Moorgate–Winchmore Hill

Route 625, together with 623, ran through Epping Forest *en route* to Woodford, offering one of the most scenic journeys operated by London trolleybuses. Following this conversion trolleybuses operated a greater mileage than the trams.

July saw trolleybuses replace trams at Hampstead depot, bringing them to Hampstead Heath and Parliament Hill Fields. The following services were introduced:

513	Hampstead–King's Cross–Holborn–Parliament Hill Fields *(numbered 613 in the opposite direction)*
639	Hampstead–King's Cross–Moorgate
615	Parliament Hill Fields–King's Cross–Moorgate

For these services 46 new 'J2' AECs and 'H1' Leylands were allocated to Holloway depot.

During the summer of 1938 another new class entered service in the form of 25 'J3s'. These were AEC 664Ts with BRCW bodywork and differed from the 'J2s' in being fitted with coasting and run-back brakes for use on Highgate Hill. They were numbered 1030-54 (EXV 30-54) and allocated to Holloway. The last of these vehicles, No 1054, had a BRCW body of updated design, which, in reality, was little different from its predecessors apart from having radiused top corners to the front upper-deck windows, although these were nowhere near as rounded as those on subsequent bodies from other manufacturers.

The next conversion took place in October with new routes 659 (Waltham Cross–Holborn Circus), 679 (Smithfield–Ponder's End)

and 649 (Ponder's End– Stamford Hill). Edmonton depot operated the 649 and 659 and shared the 679 with Holloway. More new trolleybuses were licensed for the introduction of these routes and comprised the last two 'H1s', 20 'J3s' and 19 buses of a new 'K' class, which would become the largest class of London trolleybus. Of these, Nos 1055-1154 and 1255-1304 (EXV 55-154, 255-304) were all-Leyland vehicles with Metrovick equipment and were classified 'K1'; Nos 1155-1254 and 1305-54 (also with matching EXV registrations) were similar vehicles but with English Electric equipment and were classified 'K2'.

The final conversion of 1938 came about on 6 November with the introduction of route 627 from Tottenham Court Road to Edmonton, seeing off the last of the trams from the former MET routes. Fifty 'Ks' were used for this conversion.

Delivered from 1938, the all-Leyland 'K1' class totalled 150 vehicles. No 1058 (EXV 58) is seen in 1960 bound for Tottenham Court Road on route 629, which at its northern extremity reached almost into rural England at Enfield Town. Classes K1 and K2 together numbered some 300 vehicles and represented the most numerous type of trolleybus delivered to London Transport. *R. H. G. Simpson*

A feature in a number of London trolleybus depots was the traverser, used to park vehicles, and in some cases a turntable was incorporated. The last one, in use until the final day of operation in 1962, existed in Isleworth depot. Seen when almost new on the traverser at Stamford Hill depot is all-Leyland 'K2' No 1202 (EXV 202).
The Omnibus Society

A prewar (1939) view oozing atmosphere, with genuine gas lamp, tram in the background and vintage van with wire wheels. Taking pride of place, however, is brand-new all-Leyland 'K2' No 1348 (EXV 348) bound for Leyton on route 555, which replaced tram 55 upon completion of conversion work at Leyton depot on 11 June. This trolleybus is now preserved by the Transport Museum Society of Ireland
The Omnibus Society

The year 1939 started brightly enough with the trolleybuses-for-trams conversion programme proceeding apace. In February 'K1s' and 'K2s' ousted trams from Stamford Hill and began operating on the following routes:

643	Wood Green–Farringdon Road–Holborn (returning via Grays Inn Road), journeys from Holborn to Wood Green later being numbered 543.
647	Stamford Hill–London Docks
683	Stamford Hill–Moorgate

In addition the 649 was extended from Stamford Hill to Liverpool Street.

In March tram route 53 was replaced by trolleybus route 653 between Tottenham Court Road and Aldgate, where trolleybuses used the newly opened bus station. 'K'-class trollies were again used for this conversion, although many were replaced after only a few months. The replacement vehicles were chassisless trolleybuses of Classes L1 and L2. The 'L2s' were direct descendants of the prototype 'L2', No 954, being built by Metro-Cammell with AEC running units, Metrovick motors and English Electric controllers. The 'L1s' were identical apart from being fitted with coasting and run-back brakes for use on Highgate Hill. The 'L1s' and 'L2s' were numbered 1355-69 (EXV 355-69) and 1370-8 (EXV 370-8) respectively.

The next vehicle numerically was probably one of the most famous of all London trolleybuses. Classified 'X5' in the experimental series and numbered 1379 (EXV 379), it was to all intents and purposes a standard 'L2'-class chassisless vehicle. However, it was intended as a prototype for trolleybuses to work through the Kingsway Subway (which had central island platforms for loading) and was therefore fitted with jack-knife doors on the offside of the rear platform, which, in turn, necessitated a straight staircase; seating capacity was reduced to 68 as a result. Although No 1379 was basically similar in

Fresh from repaint, No 1377 (EXV 377) looks strange with no advertisements adorning the front. This was one of only nine chassisless AEC/Metro-Cammell Class L2 vehicles delivered in 1939, the first (No 954) having appeared in 1938. However, the success of this construction method led to the longest continuous delivery (Nos 1355-1529) of London trolleybuses. Note the by now disused route-number stencil-holder on the rear offside of the vehicle. *F. G. Reynolds*

appearance to the 'Ls', the rear profile was much more upright and there were only five windows on the offside of the lower deck, the rearmost being replaced by an unglazed panel. An indicator for displaying 'Kingsway' was fitted to the front dome; this was never used in service, nor were the offside doors, but neither was removed, and the bus remained in its original condition throughout its life, which was spent at Holloway.

At about the same time that the 'L1s' and 'L2s' were delivered the last trams were withdrawn from Walthamstow and Leyton depots and all but two routes from Hackney. 'K1s' and 'K2s' were drafted in for the replacement trolleybus services, which were as follows:

555	Leyton–Bloomsbury
557	Chingford Mount–Liverpool Street
581	Woodford–Bloomsbury

These replaced tram routes 55, 57 and 81 and were numbered in the 5xx series because route numbers 655 and 657 were already in use.

In May 1939 another experimental vehicle arrived. This was classified 'X7', although the 'X6' vehicle would not arrive for another six months. No 1671 was an all-Leyland chassisless

vehicle with Metrovick equipment and had actually been completed in February; between then and its arrival in London it had been used by Leyland Motors Ltd as a demonstrator, hence its Lancashire registration (DTD 649). It would remain unique in being the only trolleybus bought by London Transport not registered in London.

To the layman, No 1671 must at first glance have looked as if its body had been fitted the wrong way round, for, instead of the usual double wheels at the back, it was fitted with twin-steer front axles and a single axle at the rear. Even internally it was back-to-front, with the longitudinal seats at the front of the lower deck. The idea of this arrangement was to improve the vehicle's turning circle and to reduce tyre wear caused by the rigid rear bogie. In service the steering also proved to be lighter, but, in spite of its advantages, No 1671 remained unique, running in normal service from Fulwell and (later) Hanwell depots.

Delivery of two more new classes began in the summer of '39. The 'L3s' were more chassisless vehicles built by Metro-Cammell with AEC running units but with both motors and controllers by Metrovick. The class eventually totalled 150 buses, being numbered 1380-1529 and starting a new registration sequence as FXH 381-529, No 1380 being the odd-man-out as FXF 380. The second type was Class N1, which began arriving in dribs and drabs during the summer.

Also in course of delivery at this time were the 'Ns'. These marked a return to the conventional chassis and body, the former being the familiar AEC 664T, and the bodywork shared between BRCW (90 vehicles) and Park Royal (25). The BRCW version was classified 'N1', the Park Royal 'N2'. The BRCW bodies were much the same as that on No 1054, the final 'J3', with the slightly radiused front upper-deck windows. A few 'N1s' had been delivered in June 1939, but they didn't really come on stream until September-October. Given fleetnumbers 1555-1644 (FXH 555-644), they were delivered over the course of a year, the last arriving in June 1940.

On 3 September 1939 Neville Chamberlain announced that, following Hitler's invasion of Poland, Britain was at war with Germany and effectively put an end to London Transport's 'trolleybuses for trams' conversion programme, although this was quite possibly not the sole reason for the Führer's actions! At the time there remained in service some 1,100 trams, operating over 134 miles of track.

Despite the declaration of war, outstanding orders continued to be honoured. Thus in November came the first of the production

◀ It had been the intention to convert the South London tram routes to trolleybus, but use of the infrastructure in the Kingsway Subway would have required modifications to trolleybuses to enable passengers to embark and disembark on the island platforms. Class X5 No 1379 (EXV 379) should have been the 11th 'L2' but was built with offside rear door and with rearmost offside lower-deck window blanked off. Although the tunnel experiments were not a success, No 1379 would lead a normal life until withdrawn in 1955 on the basis of being non-standard. *C. Carter*

In 1939, when the first chassisless AEC/Metro-Cammell 'L3s' ventured into service, few could have anticipated that vehicles of this class would be the last trolleybuses operating in London. No 1426 (FXH 426), in Kingston town centre on 14 April 1962, has suffered a de-wirement. Such occurrences were comparatively unusual and seldom photographed. No 1426 is seen on the local route 602 with a late Austin Seven and Ford Prefect 100E to its right. *A. D. Packer*

With the 'L'-class chassisless trolleybuses came bodywork with rounded treatment of the upper-deck windows, giving a much more pleasing appearance. Class L3 No 1436 (FXH 436) is seen at Wimbledon Town Hall on the very last night — 8 May 1962. One wonders how many passengers realise that this is the last time they will travel on such a silent form of transport. *John Bishop*

'M1s'. Like the prototype, No 953, they were of unit construction, being built jointly by AEC and Weymann to an AEC design, as described on page 25. They were numbered 1530-54 (FXH 530-54).

The 25 'N2s', most of which arrived in November 1939, were a very different kettle of fish from the 'N1s' and the 'E3s' (the only other class to be bodied by Park Royal). The 'E3s' had been barely distinguishable from the contemporary Leyland- and BRCW-bodied vehicles, with straight window louvres. On the 'N2' the front upper-deck windows were heavily radiused at the top and, on the front side windows, the lower corners as well; the 'E3' was identifiable by its thick front corner pillars, but those on the 'N2' were thicker still, making it easily distinguishable. The 'N2' also had a divided rear dome with a horizontal strip at the top of upper-deck window level; the front rainshields were flatter, following more closely the contours of the windows. Internally too the 'N2' was like no other London trolleybus, having rounded window pillar covers as used on the RT and on the T-class coach, although these were fitted to the 'N2s' because it had become

The Weymann-bodied AECs of Class M1 were of unit (rather than the by now familiar chassisless) construction and entered service after the outbreak of World War 2. As apparent from this official Weymann photograph of No 1531 (FXH 531) at Addlestone, they differed very little in appearance from the 'L' classes. *Glyn Kraemer-Johnson collection*

With wartime markings on the front mudguards and with blanked headlights, 'L3' No 1526 and 'N2' No 1668 stand at Barking when almost new. *C. F. Klapper / The Omnibus Society*

standard Park Royal practice, rather than a specification of London Transport.

It will be recalled that the previous (and only other) batch of Park Royal-bodied trolleybuses suffered a premature end to their working lives due to the inferior quality of their bodies. Although most managed to last out until Stage 13 of trolleybus abandonment, in January 1962, many of the 'N2s', surprisingly, had developed sagging waistlines; surprisingly, because Park Royal was to become one of the major builders of London bus bodies, including many hundreds of RTs and RTLs and almost all the Routemasters, many of which remain in service after 40 years without showing the weaknesses apparent in the trolleybuses.

▼ Harlesden's Jubilee clock has served as a backdrop in many views; here Class N1 No 1619 (FXH 619) — one of 90 BRCW-bodied AECs delivered in 1939 after hostilities had begun — swings round on route 666 to Hammersmith in 1961. The Ford Thames Trader to the left is long forgotten, as is the traditional British Home Stores frontage. *C. Carter*

The war — now being termed the 'Phoney War' because of the lack of effect on those at home in Britain — had not been without its effect on London's trolleybus system, blackout regulations having been introduced immediately. Headlamps were masked, while the front edges of front mudguards and the lower edge of the rear platform wall were painted white to aid visibility; a solid white circle was painted on the rear of motor buses so that trolleybus drivers could tell which buses they could safely overtake at night. Internally, every other light bulb was removed from the saloons, but, after a short while, a shade was developed

Following the outbreak of hostilities, London Transport's task remained to keep the capital moving, although this was somewhat easier with the almost-new trolleybuses than with the inherited tram and ageing motor-bus fleets. With blackout regulations in force, night-time visibility was aided by painting corners and rears white, as on Class F1 No 714 (DLY 714). *A. B. Cross*

On the 698 route there remained a constant reminder of past glories in the form of the Erith Council Tramways depot. Class H1B Leyland/East Lancs No 790B (ELB 790) passes en route to Woolwich in the 1950s. New in 1938 with a Metro-Cammell body, this vehicle was another war casualty and was rebodied in 1946. *C. Carter*

which allowed more light internally but was less visible from the outside, and this was adopted as standard. Despite these precautions, the trolleybus must have been more visible from the air by virtue of the vivid blue flashes that emanated from the overhead and about which little could be done.

In an effort to lessen the danger to passengers from flying glass, anti-blast netting was fitted to all side windows (except for the opening portion of half-drops), with a small diamond shape left through which the passenger was intended to ascertain his whereabouts.

A further tram-to-trolleybus conversion took place on 5 November 1939, tram route 61 being replaced by trolleybus 661 (Aldgate–Leyton) and tram 63 by the 663 (Aldgate–Ilford), using the newly delivered 'N1s' and 'N2s'. On 10 December 'J3s' and 'L1s' began operating on route 611 (Highgate Village–Moorgate), both types being fitted with coasting and run-back brakes for use

on Highgate Hill. This replaced tram route 11 and operated from Holloway depot. Holloway (later Highgate) depot retained the rest of its tram routes until 1952, operating trams and trolleybuses side by side during this time.

Apart from the introduction of rationing, nothing much had changed by the beginning of 1940, a handful of new trolleybuses being delivered to London Transport in the form of 'L3s', 'M1s' and 'N2s'. Also delivered at this time was yet another experimental vehicle, classified 'X6' and numbered 1670 (FXH 670). This was another chassisless vehicle, built this time by English Electric with AEC running units. The design of No 1670 differed in technical detail from other chassisless buses and made for a more rigid construction. The front bulkhead was set further back, resulting in a longer front side window and the loss of two seats. It was in fact built to English Electric's own design but differed little from the London standard, although it retained straight window louvres at the front of the upper deck, with slender corner pillars which, in this writer's opinion, looked somehow more elegant than the radiused corners. It bore a strong resemblance to the Leyland product. Badly damaged during the war, it would be rebuilt by Weymann, which fitted it with a new top deck with radiused front windows, giving it an appearance similar to that of the 'M1s'.

On the international front Germany invaded the Low Countries, and the flotilla of 'little ships' rescued some 330,000 servicemen from Dunkirk. Meanwhile all was quiet on the trolleybus front, with nothing happening until June 1940, when the last tram-to-trolleybus conversion took place. This stage of the programme focused on Poplar, which had been enlarged for the purpose, and West Ham. These two depots provided trolleybuses for the following new routes:

565	Holborn–East Ham
567	Aldgate–West Ham
665	Bloomsbury–Barking

'L3s' and 'M1s' were used for the conversion, after which a few more 'L3s', 'N1s' and a solitary 'N2' were delivered before supplies dried up for a while.

Bombing of London had started in the summer but in early September the Blitz began in earnest. With the ensuing loss of life, homes and industry the damage and disruption caused to the trolleybus network seems incidental. Bombing of the Docks area continued night after night for 76 nights with only one exception (brought about by bad weather). Those of us too young to

remember or to have lived through it can only try to imagine the horror and the fear and to marvel at the courage of those East Enders who faced up to the situation and carried on as normally as possible. No doubt in many countries the same situation would have seen long lines of refugees leaving the danger zone; not in London. However, this book is about the trolleybus, and so on trolleybuses we must concentrate, not that their operation was without its share of tragedy and bravery. On the very first night of the Blitz trolleybus No 1565 had its body damaged beyond repair and many others followed during the next two months. In all cases it was possible to salvage the chassis, which were rebodied at a later date.

One of the most serious and disruptive events took place in November 1940, when Bexley depot received bomb damage resulting in the total destruction of four trolleybus bodies. Again, the chassis were saved and later received new bodies. It is amazing how few trolleybuses were totally destroyed, the majority of damaged vehicles being rebodied, no matter how hopeless they looked — something which seemed far less common with the motor-bus fleet.

Disruption of services by bomb craters and fallen buildings was considerable, especially during the Blitz, and here the weakness of the trolleybus — its inability to stray from the overhead — was brought to the fore. Whereas the motor bus could be diverted through nearby streets, the trolleybus was useless when deprived of its power supply, except for the very short distances it was able to cover under battery power. However, full credit must be given to the emergency services and LT staff who dealt with these instances, not only rapidly but frequently in record time. There were instances, where damage to the roadway or removal of debris could not be carried out immediately, of temporary wiring being erected to enable trolleybuses to operate a diverted section of route. Tramway staff were also given powers to demolish and remove damaged buildings where their dangerous condition was impeding services.

Isolated incidents of bomb damage continued throughout the system, and late 1940 the shortage of vehicles was becoming a problem. Throughout the war, bus operators in seaside towns found themselves with buses to spare, due to falling traffic brought about by the lack of holidaymakers and the restriction of movement in coastal towns, and were thus able to loan vehicles to more hard-pressed operators. In the instance of London's trolleybus shortage, it was Bournemouth Corporation that came to the rescue, 18 of its smart yellow-and-brown Sunbeams arriving

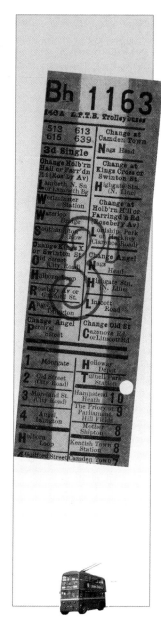

in the capital. These were six-wheelers, with a mixture of Park Royal and English Electric bodies built to Bournemouth's standard layout with separate entrance and exit, and were sent to Ilford for routes 691 and 693.

In October 1940 a trickle of new vehicles began to arrive once more. First to be delivered were 11 of a new 'K3' class. Like the 'K2s', they were all-Leyland products with Metrovick motors and English Electric controllers; in fact the only visible difference was that the sidelights were built into the front panels rather than being side-mounted. Numbered 1672-96, the 'K3s' started a new registration series as GGP 672-96, which to the authors somehow never seemed quite trolleybus-like, for some reason.

January 1941 saw the arrival of the first of another new class, namely Class P1. Again these were Leylands, similar in chassis specification to the 'K3s' but bodied by Metro-Cammell. They showed no signs of austerity, being built to prewar standards, their curvaceous contours exaggerated by their radiused front windows; indeed, they were very similar in appearance to the

'L3s'. They were delivered in dribs and drabs over some 10 months and were given fleetnumbers 1697-1721, again with corresponding GGP registrations.

The last of the 'P1s', which were also the last new trolleybuses to prewar design, was delivered at the same time as the first of the rebodied war-damaged vehicles. Sixteen of these chassis had been rebodied by Weymann, basically to prewar design but with important differences brought about by the shortage of materials. The most noticeable external difference was the use of sliding ventilators instead of the usual half-drops. The upper deck showed a foretaste of what was to come when the Ministry of Supply 'utility' designs were introduced, having single-skin roofs and side panelling. Strangely (and in complete contrast) the last five had luxurious lower saloons featuring Alhambrinal ceilings; these consisted of textured panels in cream, each being lined out in green and brown. The explanation for this oddity may have been that Weymann had the panels in stock, having used them fairly recently on both trolleybuses and motor buses for

Peace eventually returned to London, although trolleybuses such as Metro-Cammell-bodied Leyland 'P1' No 1719 (GGP 719), one of a class of just 25 delivered in 1940, served to remind us of those dark days. To the left in this view taken on 11 April 1959 at Waltham Cross is all-Leyland 'K2' No 1190 (EXV 190). *Alan B. Cross*

Bournemouth and Brighton. The panelling looked fine when new but quickly became dingy, especially at night. The new bodies were of composite (rather than all-metal) construction — the first of this type to be delivered to London Transport, although the trolleybuses inherited from the LUT had been built in this way. Two of the buses dealt with in this manner had originally been short-wheelbase 60-seaters but had had their chassis lengthened before being rebodied with standard 70-seat bodies.

The rebodied trolleybuses retained their original fleetnumbers but were given an 'A' suffix, which was also added to the classification; thus 'D2' No 406 became 'D2A' No 406A. (By as early as 1950 these buses would be showing signs of stress — common in wartime-built bodies, due to the use of poor-quality materials, particularly unseasoned wood — and were sent to Mann Egerton of Norwich, which carried out a rebuilding programme that involved fitting new timber and replacing staircases.)

Receipt of the rebodied buses, together with the 'K3s' and 'P1s', eased the vehicle shortage sufficiently for nine Sunbeams to be returned to Bournemouth in November 1941, the rest staying until September 1942.

Although the tram-replacement scheme had been halted, and new routes and extensions were few and far between, a new service was started in October 1944, this being the 695 from Chadwell Heath to Bow Church.

Every cloud, they say, has a silver lining, and, whatever the dangers, discomforts and hardships brought about by the war, it must have been a particularly interesting time for enthusiasts, especially bearing in mind there were no enthusiasts' publications. Usually the first they knew about a particular development was when they saw it with their own eyes. One wonders what their reactions were to the next new trolleybuses to be delivered to London Transport, the first of which arrived in November 1944. These had Leyland six-wheel chassis and Metro-Cammell bodywork, but there ended any resemblance to the standard London trolleybus. No 1722 was the first of 43 trolleybuses intended for South Africa which had been diverted to London, partly to help with the Board's vehicle shortage but mainly because of the high risk of shipping them abroad due to German U-boat attacks.

The 12 'SA1s' and 13 'SA2s' were intended for Durban and, like the 'SA3s' that were to follow, were built to a width of 8ft — 6in wider than was permitted in this country. Special permission had therefore to be obtained for them to operate, whereafter they

were sent to the quieter and less congested area of Ilford, where they remained throughout their working lives. The only difference between the 'SA1s' and 'SA2s' was that the 'SA1s' had electrical equipment by GEC whilst that in the 'SA2s' was by Metrovick. The 'SA1s' were numbered 1722-33 (GGW 722, GLB 723-33), the 'SA2s' following as 1734-46 (GLB 734-46).

The 'SA1s' and 'SA2s' were probably the most austere of all London trolleybuses in appearance, although this was probably due to the design specified by Durban rather than any wartime restrictions. They had square-cornered windows with straight rainshields, these being deeper at the front than at the sides. The lower edge of the windscreen was level with that of the side windows, which allowed the cream band to be carried around the front of the vehicle, emphasising its extra width and its square appearance. Originally they were fitted with sliding front doors, but these were panelled over before entry into service, and a seat for two was fitted inside the door well. Opening windows were fitted to all main bays, the opening portion being of tinted glass as protection from the South African sun; as such problems were rarely encountered in Ilford, half the windows were locked in the

▲ Destined always to remain at the eastern extremity of London's trolleybus network were the 8ft-wide vehicles diverted from South Africa after hostilities had begun. Intended for Durban, 'SA1' No 1723 (GLB 723), a Metro-Cammell-bodied Leyland, clearly shows the sealed front exit door while on route 693 in the late 1950s.
A. D. Packer

closed position. The destination display consisted of a single-
aperture box in which route number, intermediate points and
ultimate destination were all shown on one blind; perhaps
surprisingly, this was never altered.

Internally, too, the 'SA1s' and 'SA2s' differed markedly from
the London standard, with polished-wood window surrounds in
place of the usual rexine beloved of London Transport. Seats were
covered in brown leather instead of the usual moquette, and there
was a rearward-facing seat for three against the front bulkhead.

The 'SA3' class, originally destined for Johannesburg,
consisted of 18 8ft-wide AECs with Metro-Cammell bodywork
and English Electric equipment — a combination familiar enough
(the extra width aside) to London Transport, but again there were
many non-standard features. The bodies were similar to those of
the Leyland vehicles but were given a superficially more
'London-like' appearance by having rounded louvres over the
front windows and separate front route-number and destination
boxes, although both were much smaller than the London
standard. Again, the cream band continued beneath the
windscreen, and, like the Durban buses, they had a divided rear
emergency window. They also had front exits but with jack-knife
doors, and these too were panelled over. Internally the 'SA3s'
featured varnished-wood window surrounds and leather-covered
seats, this time in dark red. The seats themselves were even more
unlike the standard, having curved top rails that dipped between
the seating positions (those 'bra-shaped' seats again). Numbered
1747-64 (GLB 747-64), the 'SA3s' joined their South African
colleagues at Ilford, where they remained until withdrawal.

Delivery of the 'SA3s' — the last London trolleybuses ordered prewar, albeit not by LT — was completed in 1943. Fortunately, damage to vehicles seemed to subside around this time, although No 953, the prototype 'M1', was completely destroyed and subsequently scrapped. This, however, was due to an electrical fire and not enemy action. The 'peace' was to be short-lived, however, and in 1944 Germany began to use its V1 flying bombs (could have been a trolleybus classification!), or 'doodlebugs', as they became known, with some serious effects on the trolleybus system.

Probably the worst incident of the war occurred in June 1944, when Bexleyheath depot, which had already sustained damage in 1940, received a direct hit from a 'doodlebug'. The attack occurred in the early hours of 29 June, when the depot was full. The building caught fire, and every one of the 84 trolleybuses

inside was rendered unserviceable. Twelve were completely destroyed, 26 had their bodies damaged to such an extent that they had to be scrapped (although the chassis were rebodied after the war), and the remainder suffered damage sufficient to stop them entering service that day. Miraculously, despite this devastation, a near-normal service was in operation by the following evening, reflecting the spirit of those who refused to be beaten and who moved trolleybuses into the area from all over the network so that services should not be disrupted for any longer than was absolutely necessary. This must have been a bonus for the enthusiast, Bexleyheath routes being worked by types never seen in the area before or since.

As if the Bexleyheath incident wasn't bad enough, in the following month West Ham works and canteen suffered badly from hits in two separate raids on the Docks, just a week apart.

◀ Class SA3 comprised 18 Metro-Cammell-bodied AECs intended for Johannesburg. Their destination boxes were different from those of the Durban examples, being more restricted, as can be seen from this view of 'SA3' No 1759 (GLB 759); the front door is again sealed, and the bottom panelled over. Being less square in appearance, these vehicles were more attractive than the 'SA1s' and 'SA2s'.
J. Wills / LCC Tramways Trust

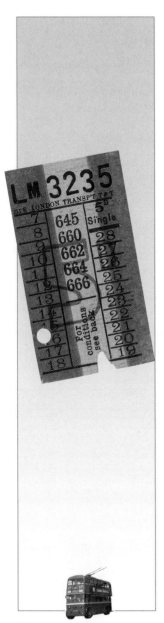

This time one trolleybus was totally destroyed and a further 18 lost their bodies. These included No 1001A, already rebodied by Weymann after an earlier attack, but you can't keep a good trolleybus down: the chassis subsequently received a third body, this time by East Lancs, and lived on to fight another day. As mentioned earlier, the English Electric chassisless vehicle, No 1670, had its upper deck damaged and later received a new roof by Weymann.

Although the Bexleyheath and West Ham incidents had caused an enormous amount of damage and disruption, there had been no loss of life. Trolleybus-wise, the most horrific event of the war occurred shortly after the first West Ham attack, on 27 July, when trolleybus No 1387 received a direct hit from a flying bomb during the evening peak; it was completely destroyed, with a heavy death toll.

By the autumn of 1944 the tide of the war had turned such that LT was able to send further reconditioned war-damaged chassis for rebodying. Orders were placed for 45 new bodies — 25 from East Lancs at Blackburn and 20 from Northern Coachbuilders at Newcastle. Recipients of East Lancs bodies were given a 'B' suffix to their fleetnumbers and classification codes, whilst those rebodied by Northern Coachbuilders received a 'C'. Other rebuilding work was undertaken by a variety of firms, including Beadle and Park Royal, as well as by Charlton Works and Fulwell depot.

Both East Lancs and Northern Coachbuilders were well-known bodybuilders, but neither had previously supplied vehicles to London Transport (although, before it began rebodying the trolleybuses, NCB had built some bodies on new Guy chassis under contract to Park Royal). East Lancs had never previously built bodies for London (and would not do so again for many years).

The East Lancs trolleybus bodies were of all-metal construction and were basically to the standard prewar design, although the front upper-deck windows were pure East Lancs, both top corners of each window being radiused. Internally, they fell below the usual standard, having painted (rather than rexine-covered) side panels. East Lancs rebodied two of the unit-construction 'M1s', which had additional chassis frames fitted, whilst chassisless 'L3' No 1385 was given a proper chassis and reclassified 'N1B' — shades of the old broom with the new brush and handle! Wranglings over price meant that 3½ years elapsed between receipt of the first and last East Lancs rebodies.

The Northern Coachbuilders bodies were of composite construction — again, basically to the prewar design — but could be easily identified by the curved rainshields over the front upper-deck windows. In common with the East Lancs bodies, they had fixed nearside windscreens. Among the chassis sent to NCB were two of the Class B2s, which were lengthened before being given 70-seat bodies. Delivery from the Tyneside company was much more prompt, all 20 bodies being completed by September 1946.

Between them, East Lancs and Northern Coachbuilders rebodied 29 Leylands and 16 AECs. All the Leylands were put to work on the Bexley routes, which became renowned for their high content of rebodied trolleybuses; the AECs went to West Ham and Holloway.

Throughout the war London Transport had been experimenting with what were to become known nationally as 'pay as you enter' vehicles but which the Board preferred to call 'pay as you board' (PAYB). There had been various trials with converted STLs and RT19, and in 1945 it became the turn of the Trolleybus Department. The first experiment had involved the conversion of an STL to centre-entrance, and it was decided to use the same layout for the first PAYB trolleybus. Here the Trolleybus Department had a head start, for it already had a centre-entrance trolleybus in the shape of No 61, the 1933 prototype. Some alteration was necessary, notably the fitting of a full-width front bulkhead and a consequent rearrangement of the lower-deck seating to allow a larger area for passengers to stand whilst waiting to pay their fares. All the London PAYB experiments involved a seated conductor, and in the case of No 61 a tip-up seat was provided, which was almost under the stairs. In front of this was a desk on which was placed a rather cumbersome cash register. Tickets were issued from a normal TIM machine. A periscope was fitted so that the conductor could keep a check on the number of vacant upper-deck seats. The original air-operated doors were retained.

No 61 re-entered service on the 604 from Fulwell depot in March 1945, a few days after the trials with STL1753 had ended. The motor bus had proved to be slower in service than a conventional vehicle, and the same was found to be true of No 61; the platform was not large enough for all intending passengers to board before paying their fare, and this resulted in delays at stops. The trials ended in October 1945, and the bus duly reverted to conventional operation.

For the second experiment, begun while No 61 was still on trial, it was decided to use a rear-entrance vehicle. The choice of bus was arbitrary in as much as the trolleybus used, No 378, was in need of repair after suffering damage from a flying bomb. The rear end of this bus was considerably rebuilt, having the platform built up to floor level, making a standing area for passengers waiting to pay their fare. A corner pillar was built on the platform, enabling jack-knife doors to be fitted, which in turn necessitated the inclusion of an emergency exit, fitted in the centre of the rear wall. The rear bulkhead was narrowed and the nearside longitudinal seat reduced in length to accommodate just two. The staircase was rebuilt, being moved forward and now turning through 180°; as a result the offside longitudinal seat was also shortened, to seat three, reducing the overall capacity to 66. All this to increase the circulating area. The conductor's tip-up

seat was again positioned beneath the stairs, giving him an excellent view of the platform and doorway. Again he was given a cash desk with till and tickets were issued from a TIM machine.

No 378 followed No 61 onto the 604, operating from December 1945 until March 1946 and resulting in the same dismal failure as its predecessors. The PAYB idea faded into oblivion until the late 1960s, when it was suddenly decided that delays at stops and inconvenience to passengers no longer mattered. No 378 was rebuilt as a 68-seater, losing its platform doors but retaining its high platform and two entrance steps. It worked spasmodically from Walthamstow before being demoted to driver-training duties and was scrapped in 1954.

◄ When Class C3 No 378 (CUL 378) was delivered in 1936 no one could have envisaged the rebuilding that would take place in 1945. The rear platform was rebuilt, and a lower offside window at the rear was panelled over to facilitate a 'Pay As You Board' experiment whereby the conductor sat taking fares. The experiment was not a success, and No 378 saw out the rest of its days on learner duties, being withdrawn in 1954.
F. G. Reynolds

As is well-known, the war in Europe came to an end in May 1945, whereupon began the long struggle for a return to normality. The first move as far as London's trolleybuses were concerned was the Board's receipt of quotations for new vehicles to replace the ageing 'Diddlers'.

After the war any resumption of the tram-to-trolleybus conversion seemed unlikely, at least in the foreseeable future, and this view was reinforced when the Board announced that all remaining trams were to be overhauled and renovated. Even more doom-laden was a further announcement, later in 1946, that the motor bus was thought to be more suitable than the trolleybus and would be used to replace the remaining trams.

In the years following the cessation of hostilities bus travel reached an all-time peak, unfortunately at a time when operators were having to cope with fleets of ageing vehicles long overdue for withdrawal, which had been poorly maintained during the war years. The London trolleybus fleet wasn't too bad in this respect; as already mentioned, the rebodied war-damaged vehicles were returning to the fleet and, apart from the 'Diddlers' and the experimental prototypes, no trolleybus was more than 11 years old.

Some signs of standardisation between the motor-bus and trolleybus fleets became apparent in 1946, when it was decided that use of the Johnson typeface, standard on the former for destination blinds etc, should be extended to the trolleybus fleet. This style of lettering has always been considered to be one of the most legible and attractive and is still in use today, but, for some strange reason, it never seemed to suit the trolleybus blinds. After the chunky route numbers and lettering that had been standard for so long, the Johnson script appeared 'spindly', and the spacing of the wording went haywire. 'Via' points were condensed unnecessarily, leaving large expanses of blank blind, whilst other lettering was spaced so far apart that it disappeared beyond the edges of the destination screen.

As a result of the quotations received, an order had been placed for 77 new trolleybuses to replace the 60 'Diddlers' and the 17 buses lost during the war. Following experiments in the Hampton Court area with a trolleybus bound for South Africa (the scenic route?), it was decided that these should be 8ft wide.

Classified 'Q1', the first of these arrived in February 1948. Based on BUT chassis (BUT — British United Traction —

being a collaboration between AEC and Leyland for building trolleybuses), they were built at Leyland's plant near Kingston-upon-Thames and had English Electric controllers and 120hp Metrovick motors, making them much more powerful than anything used hitherto in London. Bodywork was by Metro-Cammell and was clearly based very much on the prewar design. There were differences, however, apart from the extra width, the most noticeable being their five-bay construction. The opening windows were at last brought into line with current motor-bus practice, having winding gear instead of the unreliable spring-loaded type, which had a habit of tipping sideways and jamming in the half-open position. There was no front grille, and the nearside windscreen was fixed (as on the later rebodies). The design and finish of these vehicles proved once again how separate the Tram & Trolleybus Department was from the motor-bus section; one might have expected the postwar trolleybus to be a sort of electric RT (what a lovely thought!), but there were very few similarities between the two types, although the 'Q1s' did feature standard LT moquette.

The first batch of 'Q1s' was numbered 1765-1841 and registered HYM 765-841. They were an immediate success with crews and public alike, being fast, smooth and comfortable. As intended, they were used to replace the 'Diddlers', most of which were scrapped, although some of the latter went on to become driver trainers in parts of the system foreign to them. No 1, of course, joined the LT heritage collection at Reigate garage.

A month before the arrival of the first 'Q1s', on 1 January 1948, the London Passenger Transport Board ceased to exist, being replaced by the London Transport Executive and becoming part of the nationalised British Transport Commission, although it was never subject to the restrictions of vehicle suppliers imposed on other BTC companies. Indeed, the only visible sign of change was to the legal lettering carried on the vehicles.

Since the outbreak of war, the motor-bus fleet had undergone a number of livery changes, but the trolleybuses retained their original livery throughout, apart from experiments in 1938-39: at the outbreak of hostilities (in common with the motor buses) their silver roofs were repainted matt brown as a camouflage measure, although on trolleybuses the brown started from the first bay, the dome being left red. Although, postwar, the motor buses received

new liveries with red or green roofs, the trolleybus roofs remained brown until the end.

The year 1950 proved to be a significant one for electric traction in London. In July, the Tram & Trolleybus Department ceased to be a separate entity and was merged with the Central Area bus fleet to form Central Road Services. One of the first visible signs of this came when the trolleybuses began to carry garage-code plates, having hitherto displayed only a running number. At the same time, a number of depots were renamed, as follows:

Old name	New name
Hackney	Clapton
Hendon	Colindale
Holloway	Highgate
Hounslow	Isleworth
Leyton	Lea Bridge
Sutton	Carshalton

A rear-nearside view of 'Q1' No 1802 (HYM 802) when almost new, showing the thought put by the design team into making this a superb-looking vehicle. Designers frequently run out of ideas with rear treatments, but here they have enhanced the glory days of London's trolleybuses.
The Omnibus Society

This was also the year in which the tram-replacement programme recommenced in earnest. First to go were the trams operating from Wandsworth. This depot also operated some trolleybuses, on the 612 and 630 routes; when the trams were withdrawn, approval was given for trolleybus route 612 to be replaced by motor-bus route 44, whilst the 630 workings were transferred to Hammersmith, thus removing electric traction from Wandsworth. The die was cast.

By this time the future of the trolleybus in London was uncertain, to say the least, but there were as yet no public plans for its replacement. A number of the older trolleybuses were showing their age, and it was decided to order a further 50 'Q1s' for delivery in 1952. Identical to the 1948 vehicles and numbered

1842-91 (LYH 842-91), they were used to replace 'C1s' at Fulwell and Isleworth, these being dispersed to other depots. As a result, the 'B2s' and a number of 'D3s' were withdrawn and scrapped, along with the two prototypes, Nos 61 and 62. The idea of allocating all the 'Q1s' to Fulwell and Isleworth was that these buses would not become life-expired until the late 1960s, it being anticipated that this small pocket of trolleybus operation would be able to continue independently after the rest of the system had been closed. These plans never came to fruition, however, as continual cuts in services meant that more and more 'Q1s' were transferred to other depots, Hanwell in particular. In any case, when No 1891 took to the road there was little doubt in anyone's mind that it would be London's last new trolleybus.

The peak in bus travel occurred in 1950/1, and the rest of the decade would show a steady decline, due largely to the increase in private-car usage and the advent of television, the latter bringing about a reduction in family outings, particularly in the evenings. As a result, operators began to cut unremunerative routes and to reduce evening and Sunday services.

The London trolleybus fleet reached its peak, at 1,811 vehicles, in 1952, but this was not a happy year. The most noteworthy event was the death of King George VI on 6 February, but perhaps equally tragic for the transport enthusiast was the withdrawal of London's last tram on 5 July. How long, we wondered, would the once all-conquering trolleybus linger on?

From 1953 onwards not only the number of passengers carried but also the number of trolleybuses operated fell into steady decline. The Coronation of HM Queen Elizabeth II on 2 June brought about a 12% increase in passengers over a normal Monday, although reduced services were operated. This event, which saw a mammoth operation by London Transport, once again showed up the disadvantages of the trolleybuses. Motor buses were drafted in from all over the LT area to carry the crowds to and from the West End and to operate sightseeing tours over the Coronation route; the trolleybuses were tied, Cinderella-like, to their overhead and were therefore condemned to continue running their mundane daily routes and miss all the splendour and pageantry.

This book is entitled 'Glory Days', and it is felt that by the mid-1950s the glory days of London's trolleybuses were over and that it is not therefore appropriate to dwell in too much detail on the demise of the system.

The ensuing years saw the trolleybus fleet suffer a steady stream of withdrawals, which included the experimental buses 754 and 1379 and the PAYB bus 378. Most of the withdrawn trolleybuses were scrapped, but a few found new homes. In 1956 five 'C1s' were sold for further service to the Georgetown Municipal Fleet in Penang, Malaya, where they were repainted into a livery of bright red and white and fitted with additional opening windows.

The official announcement that the trolleybus system was to be abandoned was made in 1954 — the same year in which London Transport unveiled the new 64-seat Routemaster that was to

replace the trolleybus. The replacement programme was duly drawn up and the date set for its implementation was March 1959. First to go would be the 654, being the route on which the oldest trolleybuses were operating, and the isolated Bexley routes. Following this the replacement programme was to be implemented on an east-to-west basis, with newer vehicles moving westwards. However, before the actual replacement programme began, routes 664, 683 and 695 were withdrawn as part of service cuts.

The withdrawal programme proper began on time on 3 March with Bexley and Carshalton depots losing their trolleybuses. In both cases it was not, as had been expected, the Routemaster that took over but the ubiquitous RT. RTLs were used in the second stage on 14 April, when Clapton depot changed over to motor buses and Lea Bridge depot was closed.

'K2' in postwar condition: No 1342 (EXV 342) emerges from Lea Bridge depot for duty on route 581 under a nest of overhead on 11 April 1959. Right to the end of trolleybus operation, the overhead was maintained in good condition and always looked neat and tidy — a creditworthy achievement, given the complicated nature of some of the junctions. There was always criticism of the 'spider's web' in the sky, but few have complained since about telegraph wires or power cables. *A. D. Packer*

In the spring of 1961, when the entire 'Q1' class was withdrawn prematurely for sale to Spanish operators, members of the 'K1' class were moved to Isleworth, which became an all-Leyland depot. Heading for Shepherds Bush on route 657, No 1077 (EXV 77) passes a newly delivered Routemaster advertising 'Bus About' tickets at 2/6 (12½p) outside Chiswick Works.
R. H. G. Simpson

Two all-Leyland Class K1 trolleybuses bound for Hounslow arrive together at the roundabout at Chiswick, at a time when, if you missed your bus, another would soon appear. The photograph was obviously taken not long after the departure of the 'Q1s', as lead vehicle No 1144 (EXV 144) still carries a WN (Wood Green) depot code. *Photomatic Ltd*

Stage 3 took place on 18 August, involving Bow and Ilford depots; still Routemasters were not available, and RTs and RTLs were used. On the closure of Ilford, rumours abounded: some said that the 'SAs' would be transferred to replace older trolleybuses, whilst others said they had been snapped up by an overseas buyer. The rumours were probably fuelled by the fact that the buses were not moved for some months, but in the event they joined their colleagues at Cohen's yard at Colindale and were scrapped.

Stage 4, in November 1959, involved Poplar and West Ham depots, and this time Routemasters were available for the changeover. Poplar became a bus garage, while West Ham operated both types for some six months. With Walthamstow, West Ham featured again in Stage 5, which took place in February 1960: five routes were converted to motor-bus operation, but both depots continued to operate trolleybuses until April, when the remaining routes were converted under Stage 6.

Hammersmith was the next depot to be closed, in July 1960, although the building was subsequently used to house the fleet of coaches operated on behalf of BEA. Routes 626, 628 and 630 were replaced. This stage of the programme called for some careful planning by engineering staff: once the last trolleybuses had run into Hammersmith depot, they were driven off to other depots whilst overhead crews began cutting down the power lines; meanwhile, the 44 airport coaches were driven from Shepherd's Bush to Hammersmith, and, to complete the cycle, a fleet of new Routemasters had arrived at Shepherd's Bush and was being prepared for entry into service on the following morning.

The Hammersmith closure was part of Stage 7 in the programme, which also saw the demise of the 611 from Highgate;

Stage 8 was implemented in November 1960 and saw the withdrawal of routes 607 and 655, both worked by Hanwell depot. A further seven routes operated by Highgate were converted in January 1961 (Stage 9), with the final route, the 627, being withdrawn the following April; this (Stage 10) also affected Edmonton and Wood Green depots, both of which operated motor buses and trolleybuses side by side for some time. Route 609 was still partly worked by Highgate on Sundays, but using Routemasters alongside the trolleybuses from Finchley until the route was withdrawn in November 1961. Stage 11, in July, involved the conversion of the 543/643, 647 and 649, all worked by Stamford Hill depot, though with some input from Edmonton on the 649. In November, Wood Green said goodbye to electric traction in Stage 12, which also saw the first withdrawals from Finchley.

By 1962 Fulwell's routes were entirely in the hands of 'L3s', as exemplified by No 1462 (FXH 462) at a wet Hammersmith in April. Routemasters such as RM1020 behind had already taken over on the 666 at the beginning of the year, and the final curtain would fall the following month. *John Bishop*

Unlucky Stage 13 took place in freezing conditions in January 1962, when Finchley and Stonebridge became motor-bus garages and Colindale closed its doors completely.

The end came on 8 May 1962, when Isleworth and Fulwell lost their trolleybuses, the former depot closing and the latter becoming a bus garage. The routes withdrawn included the 601, the first route to be operated, 31 years before.

The various closures and conversions had drawn a mixed reaction from the public. Some passed almost without notice, although some kind of small ceremony was usually arranged, and buses carried chalked farewell slogans much as the trams had done. A few depots, such as West Ham and Poplar, made more of an attempt to mark the occasion. At both, the last trolleybus, decorated for the occasion, was accompanied by a procession of busmen carrying lighted torches and, at West Ham, by a small band. Both depots had arranged a dance and party, which were

well attended. In the case of West Ham the last trolleybus to run into the depot was 'E2' No 622, the bus that had inaugurated services in the East End; in between it had covered nearly a million miles.

It is worth noting that most of the trolleybus drivers at West Ham and Poplar, who were now required to drive motor buses, were over 60. They were given an 11-day training course followed by the motor-bus driving test. Most passed first time, and those that didn't succeeded at the second attempt. Of course, the Routemaster had an automatic gearbox, which made it simpler, but even so many drivers seemed to find it easier. As one driver remarked, 'With a trolleybus your attention has to be divided fifty-fifty between the overhead and the ground. The motor bus is simpler.' Another recalled: 'You could go over a junction a hundred times without mishap, then the next time, moving just as carefully, the poles would come off!'

Interest seemed to increase as the trolleybus routes dwindled, and Stage 13, in January 1962, drew huge crowds, despite sub-zero temperatures. The final day of trolleybus operation in London, 8 May 1962 (a date engraved on the hearts of trolleybus enthusiasts), was altogether different. 'Diddler' No 1 had been moved from Reigate Country Area garage to the Clapham Museum, but it was brought out of retirement for the occasion and headed a procession carrying specially invited guests. It was followed by 'L3' No 1521, both carrying destination blinds proclaiming 'LONDON'S LAST TROLLEYBUS — 8TH MAY 1962', together with commemorative advertisements; contrasting with the last week of the trams, no other trolleybuses carried these. The 'L3' later had the honour of being London's very last trolleybus, the final

journey being from Wimbledon to Hampton Court and Fulwell. Much of the route was lined with onlookers, and the bus was followed by a procession of cars sounding their horns and leaving the public in no doubt that something special was taking place.

No 1521 arrived at Fulwell in the early hours of 9 May amidst huge crowds, and there it all came to an end. No more would we hear the 'click and kissing' or see those six-wheel giants slide slowly and silently over the points. After 31 years of faithful service, the London trolleybus rapidly became but a memory. The overhead was quickly removed, together with most of the supporting poles, few being required as lamp standards. Today it is difficult to believe that people in their 40s have never seen a trolleybus in London service.

Rest in Peace. Having given years of faithful service at Edmonton, Nos 1676 (GGP 676), an all-Leyland Class K3, and 1712 (GGP 712), a Leyland/Metro-Cammell 'P1', both dating from 1940, await their fate in the yard of George Cohen, Colindale, in November 1961. *John Bishop*

7. WHERE HAVE ALL THE TROLLEYS GONE?

Few London trolleybuses saw further service, although mention has already been made of the five 'C1s' exported to Malaya. On their withdrawal the 'Q1s' were, of course, still youthful, and all but two were sold to Spanish operators. The exceptions were No 1768, which was preserved, and No 1841, which was scrapped. The others were allocated to nine Spanish operators, although none was converted to left-hand drive. Seven were subsequently converted to single-deckers, but the most interesting conversion was that of two into 35ft left-hand-drive motor buses with underfloor engines! With hindsight, perhaps London Transport could have carried out similar conversion — a QRML, perhaps?

It is fortunate that the abandonment of the London trolleybus system coincided with the birth of the preservation movement, although it must be said that London Transport had always had regard for its past and already had a collection of buses dating back to the B type of 1910.

Mention has already been made of 'Diddler' No 1, which, following its retirement in the Clapham Museum, now resides in the LT 'overflow' museum at Acton and can be seen on various open days throughout the year. It is still in 'as withdrawn' condition and rather fragile, but it's there for all to see.

The second trolleybus to be earmarked for Clapham was 'C2' No 260, which arrived in September 1959 but was replaced by 'K2' No 1253 in May 1961. Apparently this was partly because it was felt that the 'K2' would be easier to restore to original condition and partly because it was intended to add a 'Q1' to the collection and there would then be an example of each chassis type — AEC, Leyland and BUT. No 1253 is now to be seen in the LT Museum at Covent Garden. The 'Q1' selected proved to be 1768, which was installed at Clapham on its withdrawal. It now keeps No 1 company at Acton.

Following its eviction from Clapham, No 260 passed to the London Trolleybus Preservation Society. Beautifully restored, it operated over some of the country's last remaining trolleybus systems, until they too passed into oblivion. It was joined by 'L3' No 1521, which, in view of its significance as London's last trolleybus, was presented to the Historic Commercial Vehicle Club by scrap merchant George Cohen and now forms part of the LTPS's collection at Carlton Colville, near Lowestoft, where it can still occasionally be seen in operation. Also at Carlton Colville is 'K2' No 1201, which from 1961 until 1968 had been used as a store by a garage at Holland Park.

A few trolleybuses are preserved abroad. 'H1' No 796 is in the Paris Transport Museum, whilst 'K2' No 1348 crossed the Irish Sea to Co Wicklow, where it has been preserved by the Transport Museum Society of Ireland. Three 'Q1s', all from the 1948 delivery, are preserved in Spain — No 1836 (latterly Zaragoza No 72) privately, No 1837 (Zaragoza 73) masquerading as San Sebastian No 73 and No 1839 (Zaragoza 75) by Tranvias de Zaragoza. One expatriate 'Q1', however, returned to Great Britain in 1977: No 1812, latterly Santander–Astillero No 8, was purchased and re-imported by the British Trolleybus Preservation Society, which has since restored it to London condition, in which form it normally resides at the Trolleybus Museum at Sandtoft.

And these are all that remain of what was once the world's largest trolleybus system. Fifty years after its withdrawal the tram has returned to South West London — something that was probably quite unthinkable when the people of Croydon and Wimbledon said goodbye to their trams in the 1930s. Is it, therefore, so impossible that at some time in the future the faithful silent servant might once again be seen gliding soundlessly through the streets of London? One can but hope — and wait.

TROLLEYBUS
AND TRAM
MAP

LONDON TRANSPORT

ISSUED FREE

NUMBER 1 ·
55 BROADWAY
VICTORIA 68

TROLLEYBUS & TRAM

ROUTE MAP

With the Compliments of
LONDON TRANSPORT
55 BROADWAY, S.W.I
ABBEY 1234

JANUARY 1950

BUS MAP

CENTRAL AREA
INCLUDING TROLLEYBUSES

LONDON TRANSPORT
55 BROADWAY, S.W.I
ABBEY 1234

1961

49

Whilst South West London played host to the introduction of the first trolleybuses, by London United Tramways, another early conversion from tram to trolleybus involved the Sutton–Croydon–Crystal Palace route (trolleybus 654). Because of the very hilly nature of the area around Crystal Palace, short vehicles were specified. In 1937 two further batches of 'B'-class Leylands were delivered with bodywork by BRCW which visually differed very little from that by Brush, who bodied the first batch, Nos 64-93, such was the high degree of standardisation. With withdrawal looming ever closer, No 491 (DGY 491), seen on route 654 in Croydon in March 1959, would likely have been outlasted by the prewar Morris behind. *Michael Dryhurst*

No 489 (DGY 489), another Class B1 Leyland with BRCW body, draws away as a lady in typical 1950s flowing dress, having just alighted, waits to rush off to her destination. *G. Morant / Photobus*

No 413 (DGY 413) represents the batch of 99 Class D2 Metro-Cammell-bodied Leyland trolleybuses being delivered in November 1936. Whilst a high proportion of this class was rebodied as a result of wartime damage, No 413 remained unscathed. Route 698 in Bexleyheath has weeks to go before withdrawal in this view taken in February 1959 as it turns from Market Place into Bexleyheath Broadway. In trolleybus terms the Bexleyheath area was always an isolated outpost, with no physical connection to the rest of the system. *Alan Watkins*

In February 1959 Class D2 Metro-Cammell-bodied Leyland No 434 (DGY 434) is seen in Bexleyheath Broadway — part of the main road from London to Kent since Roman times. A study of the background reveals a culture very different from that of today, with a pushbike left by the kerb with no fear of theft, and individual shops distinguishing this thoroughfare from other high streets. *Alan Watkins*

Since this photograph was taken in February 1959 the area around Bexleyheath depot has changed very little save that the properties under construction in the background have been completed. Class D3 Leyland No 553 (DLY 553), on route 698, extols the virtues of Ben Truman, whilst the period hoarding claims that Toby is even better! *Michael Dryhurst*

With a full load on board, Woolwich-bound Metro-Cammell-bodied Leyland Class D2 No 475 (DGY 475) stands at the kerbside in Welling, Kent, on route 696 in February 1959 — just days before Stage 1 of trolleybus replacement. The window display of the Danson Salon typifies the era, as does the absence of traffic and parked cars. *Michael Dryhurst*

Pursued by a Ford Thames van in Balls Pond Road in February 1959, 'K2' No 1305 (EXV 305) was the first of the second batch of these all-Leyland vehicles. The 677 was very much an East End route, starting from West India Docks and then threading its way up to Dalston and Islington before returning south to Smithfield; an early victim of trolleybus abandonment, it would be replaced by RTL-operated bus route 277 in April 1959, just two months after this photograph was taken. Typical terraced houses are portrayed in this scene. *Michael Dryhurst*

No 1123A (EXV 123) was a wartime casualty rebuilt by Weymann to peacetime appearance; an all-Leyland of 1938, it had been damaged at Stamford Hill in November 1940. The main clue to the austerity specification is the ribbed roof and slender side pillars. Seen at Leyton Green in April 1959, it awaits departure on route 555 to Bloomsbury in Central London.
Michael Dryhurst

Examples of the early 'B' and 'C' classes were disappearing by 1959, when No 379 (CUL 379) — one of 100 'C3s' with BRCW bodywork on AEC chassis new in 1936 — was photographed at Manor House on route 623 from Woodford. *Michael Dryhurst*

Deep in Hackney, Class J2 No 1000 (EXX 10), one of a batch of 75 BRCW-bodied AECs dating from 1938, pulls away from the bus stop, with ladies suitably covered for the cold February morning in 1959. Whatever the topic of conversation, it is unlikely to have concerned No 1000's odd registration. *Michael Dryhurst*

Bound for Wood Green Underground station on route 643, No 1211 (EXV 211), an all-Leyland Class K2 of 1938, stands at traffic lights in Shoreditch in June 1960, the wet conditions somehow accentuating the sombre aspect of the area, typical of those in which London's trolleybuses operated. Along with the 647, 649 and 649A, the 643 route (numbered 543 when City-bound) would succumb to the motor bus a year later, on 18 July 1961. *Michael Dryhurst*

Seen in Old Street in the City of London on route 543 to High Holborn, all-Leyland Class K2 No 1228 (EXV 228) would return to Wood Green as a 643. Travelling in the opposite direction is a new (1957) Vauxhall Victor. The near-deserted roads seem incredible when one considers that this area is nowadays subject to Congestion Charging. *Michael Dryhurst*

A rear offside view to gladden any trolleybus enthusiast's eyes, featuring Class L1 chassisless AEC/Metro-Cammell No 1361 (EXV 361). The location is Highgate Archway, with six RT-type buses and two more trolleybuses further down the road, in June 1960. Route 611, to Highgate Village, would be withdrawn the following month under Stage 7, which marked the halfway point in the trolleybus-replacement scheme; the final curtain would not fall for another two years.
Michael Dryhurst

On a bright November day in 1961, Wood Green in North London is the setting for 'M1' No 1546 (FXH 546), an AEC with Weymann bodywork — one of 25 delivered in the latter part of 1939 as unit-construction vehicles. The yellow posters on the trolleybus poles spelled the end of the Wood Green routes, including the 521, and, indeed, No 1546 would be assigned for scrap later the same month. *John Bishop*

With mere days to go before withdrawal (note the ubiquitous yellow posters on the trolleybus poles), chassisless AEC/Metro-Cammell No 1504 (FXH 504) heads for Holborn Circus through a misty Wood Green early one Sunday morning in November 1961. The lack of traffic, either on the road or parked, is eerie, to say the least, while the enthusiast recording No 1504 seems oblivious of being photographed — and maybe even of the fact that the series On the Buses was filmed in the Eastern National depot to our right! *John Bishop*

Inward-bound on route 641, all-Leyland Class K1 No 1098 (EXV 98) of 1938 pauses in an apparently deserted Wood Green to bask in the late-autumn sunshine of November 1961. Note that the overhead permits turns to either left or right, impossible in today's traffic conditions. *John Bishop*

63

No 1286 (EXV 286), an all-Leyland 'K1' delivered in early 1939, basks in the sun at Winchmore Hill in November 1961, literally days before being withdrawn from service. Route 629 had actually been abandoned six months previously, but such was the willingness of the staff that the blinds were changed from 641 to 629 especially for the photograph! *John Bishop*

An immaculate all-Leyland 'K2', No 1323 (EXV 323) of 1939, stands at the northern terminus of route 641 at Winchmore Hill; shortly it will leave the leafy suburbs for Wood Green and Moorgate. The Morris Minor, such as that seen travelling in the direction of Enfield, can still be seen on our roads today, but the trolleybus has been consigned to history. *Geoff Rixon collection*

◀◀ No 1472 (FXH 472) is showing signs of neglect and the days for route 609 are numbered as the Class L3 chassisless AEC/Metro-Cammell prepares to leave North Finchley on the long journey to Moorgate in November 1961. At this time commercial television was still a novelty, the need to advertise being evident on the vehicle. *John Bishop*

◀ Under the watchful gaze of a line of classic British cars, Class N1 No 1579 (FXH 579), a BRCW-bodied AEC built in October 1940, prepares to depart North Finchley for Canons Park on route 645 in November 1961. *John Bishop*

North Finchley was always a busy centre for trolleybuses where vehicles from Stonebridge and Colindale depots would meet with those from Finchley on routes to/from the City. 'M1' No 1540 (FXH 540), an AEC with Weymann body, has just arrived from Holborn Circus, but the blinds have already been turned for the return journey. The cycle with basket on the front (in the background) is a feature of the day now found only in working museums!
Geoff Rixon collection

Caught basking in the summer sun on route 662 at Craven Park c1960, Class N2 No 1651 (FXH 651), a BRCW-bodied AEC, was delivered in June 1940. The 'N2s' were London's last standard AEC trolleybuses, although the 'SA3s' were to follow in 1942/3.
Geoff Rixon collection

The setting sun on a cloudless November evening in 1961 seems to enhance this view of Metro-Cammell-bodied AEC 'L3' No 1497 (FXH 497) on route 645 outside Colindale depot in North London. Already many a trolleybus had passed on, to George Cohen's scrapyard behind the depot.
John Bishop

68

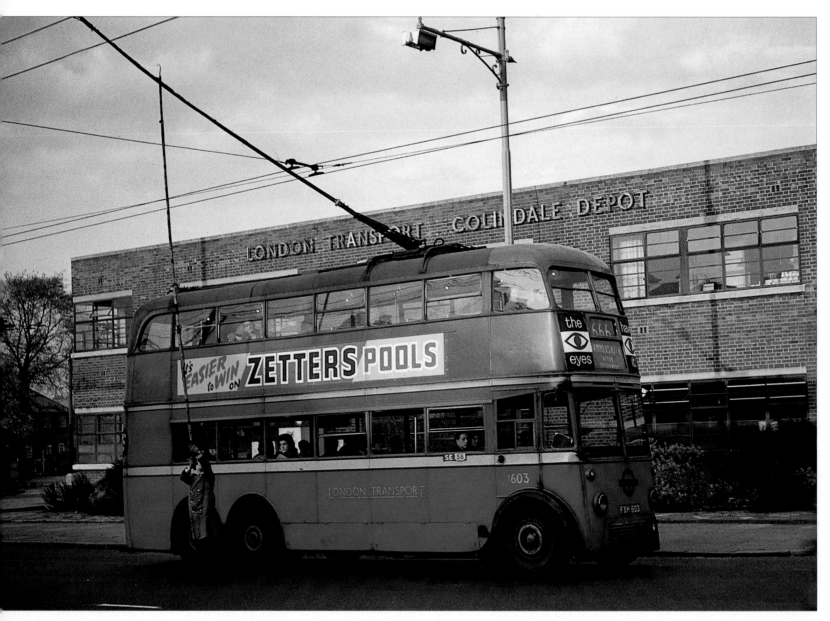

Trolleybus operation was not entirely without incident, as is apparent from this view of BRCW-bodied 'N1' AEC No 1603 (FXH 603) outside Colindale depot after losing its trolley head on the nearside boom. Swift repairs by depot staff soon had the vehicle back on its way to Hammersmith on route 666. *John Bishop*

A Class D2 Leyland trolleybus delivered in November 1936, No 461 (DGY 461) speeds away from Hammersmith trolleybus depot in February 1959. Another 16 months would elapse before the depot would close its doors to this mode of transport; however, despite its immaculate appearance, No 461 (along with the rest of its class) would be scrapped mere months after this photograph was taken. Two classic British motorcycles, one of which has the now rarely seen sidecar, jockey for a place behind. *Michael Dryhurst*

In the last few weeks of operation there would be numerous private hires covering the last areas of trolleybus operation. In April 1962 chassisless AEC/Metro-Cammell Class L3 No 1446 (FXH 446) pauses at the Wellington Road terminus in Hounslow while enthusiasts capture the vehicle on film. Both driver and conductor are smartly turned out with white caps, while the scene is completed by the duffel-coated enthusiasts on the platform!
John Bishop

Photographed in April 1962, Class L3 AEC/Metro-Cammell No 1528 (FXH 528) has entered alien territory at Hounslow (normally the preserve of Leylands from Isleworth) on another enthusiasts' special — one of many run to provide a last chance to sample the delights of this glorious system.
John Bishop

A murky day in Chiswick seems to reflect the sense of impending doom in this April 1962 view as No 1270 (EXV 270), an all-Leyland Class K2, makes its way from Shepherds Bush to Hounslow on route 657. The advertisement for cigarettes dates the scene, as does that for Chivers Jelly with 'Cheers for Chivers!' slogan. *Geoff Rixon*

Pictured on 5 May 1962, with just three days' service left, a brace of all-Leyland trolleybuses on route 657 to Shepherds Bush head across Kew Bridge on almost-deserted roads. The assertion on No 1077 (EXV 77) that 'People love Player's' would be unlikely to impress today's advertising authorities. *Geoff Rixon*

The handsome and well-proportioned lines of the 'L3' are shown to good advantage in this photograph taken at Tolworth on a gloriously sunny Sunday in April 1962, but No 1462 (FXH 462), dating from late 1939, nevertheless has only a month until final withdrawal.
John Bishop

An action view of chassisless 'L3' AEC/Metro-Cammell No 1426 (FXH 426) approaching Teddington railway bridge on route 601 bound for Twickenham. The driver on the opposite side of the road is about to take over No 1526, another 'L3', on route 605. Note the unusual style of telephone kiosk in the background.
Geoff Rixon

Kingston Bridge has long been a fine location for photographs, as may be judged from this view of No 1495 (FXH 495) in early May 1962. The Class L3 AEC is passing a period Ford Thames van, giving a true 'Sixties feel to this photograph. The trolleybus poles on Kingston Bridge would last for years after closure of the system, which was only days away. *Geoff Rixon*

The 602 route in the Surrey town of Kingston-upon-Thames was very much a local service to/from the Dittons, operating as a circular via Kingston Hill loop. No 1480 (FXH 480), a Class L3 chassisless AEC of 1939 vintage, is seen at the Dittons terminus in April 1962 extolling the virtues of Guinness! *John Bishop*

On a fine Sunday morning in April 1962, chassisless AEC/Metro-Cammell 'L3' No 1450 (FXH 450) stands outside the Red Lion, Tolworth, southern terminus of route 603; the 601 continued a short way to another terminus adjacent to the Kingston bypass. *John Bishop*

Forgotten aspects of trolleybus photography include the rear and (even more so) the re-poling of trolley booms. In May 1962 No 1444 (FXH 444), a chassisless Class L3 AEC/Metro-Cammell, engages an audience on Fulwell depot forecourt before leaving to turn left on route 604. Note the line of lights between the overhead wiring. *Geoff Rixon*

On a bright sunny day in April 1962, Hampton Wick plays host to 1939-built Class L3 No 1393 (FXH 393), one of 176 chassisless AECs bodied by Metro-Cammell, seen turning left across the River Thames over Kingston Bridge on its way to Kingston town centre. The all-conquering motor bus follows in the form of Norbiton's RT2062 on route 131. *Geoff Rixon*

With an Austin A35 in hot pursuit, 'L3' No 1419 (FXH 419) crosses the railway at Teddington on its way to Kingston in April 1962. The 605 route usually ran through to Wimbledon, but this journey is a short working terminating at Malden. *Geoff Rixon*

Their days numbered, 'L3s' 1462 (FXH 462) and 1523 (FXH 523) head the lines of trolleybuses inside Fulwell depot in April 1962. Visible in the foreground are signs of the erstwhile LUT tram tracks, which became obsolescent with the introduction of the 'Diddlers' some 31 years earlier.
Geoff Rixon

Most operators used converted buses as service vehicles, but for LT purpose-built vehicles were generally the order of the day, as demonstrated by the Leyland Cub tender at the rear of Fulwell depot in April 1962. At a moment's notice this vehicle would spring into action and attend to many a crisis at the roadside. Note the redundant London United tram track, by now disused for 31 years.
John Bishop

▲ London's final trolleybuses ran on 8 May 1962 — a date many trolleybus enthusiasts might wish to forget. Fittingly, London Transport 'resurrected' ex-LUT No 1 specially for the occasion; here the 'Diddler' is being connected to a tow vehicle for the return to its then home at the Clapham Transport Museum after conveying the Mayor and Mayoress on a commemorative tour of the Kingston-area routes. *Geoff Rixon*

▲ A superbly atmospheric view of No 1274 (EXV 274) on the last night of operation (8 May 1962) at Isleworth, showing the depot's pride and recognition of the superb service these vehicles had given. No 1274, a Class K2 Leyland, would return later in the evening with a full load of well-wishers amid scenes no doubt repeated at Fulwell. *Geoff Rixon*

▲ Headed by 'L3' No 1518 (FXH 518), this line-up of withdrawn trolleybuses at the rear of Fulwell depot on 9 May 1962 is very much a case of history repeating itself, many London United trams having met the same fate at this location. Clearly visible in this view are the brown rear domes, so painted to hide the stains caused by droplets falling from the copper overhead wires. *Geoff Rixon*

▲ George Cohen's scrapyard was located behind Colindale trolleybus depot in North London and was the last resting place for many a London trolleybus, including Nos 1309 and 1344 (EXV 309/44). Both of these fine vehicles were from Edmonton depot (EM) and were all-Leyland products built in 1938 as part of the 150-strong 'K2' class. *John Bishop*

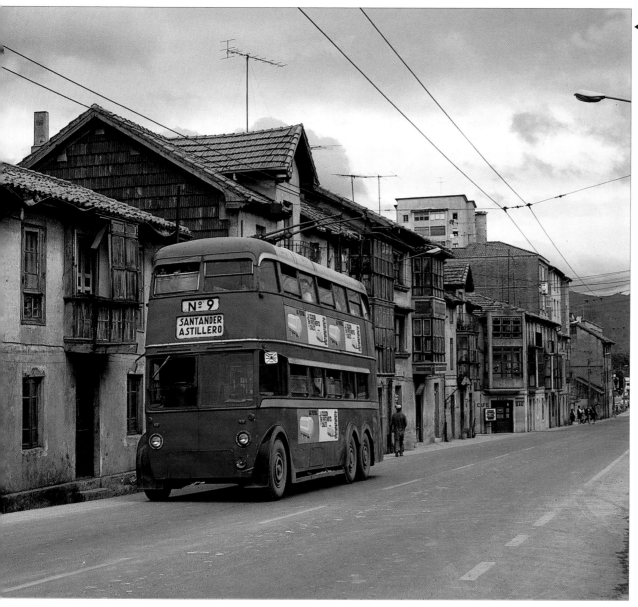

In January 1961 Class Q1 No 1883 was sold for further service in Bilbao in northern Spain. Having originally been painted in all-over red, it is seen (as Bilbao 883) in July 1973 in the later livery of red and white, in traffic conditions not dissimilar to those it would have encountered in London. *John Bishop*

The Compania de Trolebuses Santander–Astillero, in northern Spain, took six vehicles and even adopted a colour scheme similar to London Transport's. CTSA No 9, originally 'Q1' No 1781, is seen on the inter-urban route under stormy clouds in July 1973. Although it retains right-hand drive, the rear platform has been moved to the (UK) offside. *John Bishop*

▲ A Metro-Cammell-bodied AEC — one of 100 Class C2s built in 1936 — No 260 (CUL 260) benefited from enthusiasts' determination not only to preserve the vehicle but to maintain it for use on the road. Spared the usual one-way trip to George Cohen's scrapyard at Colindale, No 260 was lovingly restored and operated on private hires in Reading and Bournemouth, where it is seen at The Triangle with Bournemouth Corporation Leyland Titan PD3s. The buses on either side would see further service on the Isle of Man. *John Bishop*

▲ In May 1981 London Transport marked the 50th anniversary of the first trolleybus route by staging a rally at Fulwell depot. It is hard to believe that only 19 years had passed since the last trolleybus entered the depot, but already a generation of children had grown up not knowing the meaning of the word 'trolleybus'. No 1768 (HYM 768), an 8ft-wide Class Q1 BUT/Metro-Cammell from the London Transport collection, looks proud to be back in its rightful home. *John Bishop*

In the summer of 1990 the London Transport Collection's No 1 (HX 2756) made its way north to that Mecca for London Transport trolley enthusiasts, the East Anglia Transport Museum at Carlton Colville, near Lowestoft, Suffolk, to take part in a 'London Event' and is seen here in the company of 'C2' No 260. Regrettably, heavy rain would expose leaks in the bodywork of the 'Diddler', requiring it to be taken out of service for safety reasons. *John Bishop*

For some years the London Trolleybus Preservation Society operated No 1768 at the annual 'Trolleybus Weekend' at Carlton Colville, but the 2000 event was advertised as the last at which it would operate under power before returning to the London Transport Collection for good. In brilliant sunshine the 'Q1' is seen in service on 10 September in immaculate condition, attributable in no small part to the enthusiasm of the staff at Carlton Colville. *John Bishop*